THE HORIZON EXPERIMENT

THE HORIZON EXPERIMENT

IMAGE COMICS, INC.

Robert Kirkman: Chief Operating Officer • Erik Larsen: Chief Financial Officer • Todd McFarlane: President
Marc Silvestri: Chief Executive Officer • Jim Valentino: Executive Vice President • Eric Stephenson: Publisher/Chief Creative Officer

IMAGECOMICS.COM

THE MANCHURIAN

PORNSAK PICHETSHOTE SCRIPT
TERRY DODSON PENCILS & COLORS
RACHEL DODSON INKS
JEFF POWELL LETTERS & DESIGN
JOHN ERCEK COLOR FLATS

THE SACRED DAMNED

SABIR PIRZADA WRITER
MICHAEL WALSH ARTIST
TONI MARIE GRIFFIN
& MICHAEL WALSH COLORS
BECCA CAREY LETTERS & DESIGN

MOON DOGS

TANANARIVE DUE SCRIPT
KELSEY RAMSAY ART
JOSÉ VILLARRUBIA COLORS
JEFF POWELL LETTERS & DESIGN

MOTHERFU✪KIN' MONSTERS

J. HOLTHAM WRITER
MICHAEL LEE HARRIS ARTIST
MICAH MYERS LETTERER
JEFF POWELL ADDITIONAL DESIGN

FINDERS // KEEPERS

VITA AYALA WRITER
SKYLAR PATRIDGE ARTIST
JASON WORDIE COLOR
BECCA CAREY LETTERS & DESIGN

WILL DENNIS
PORNSAK PICHETSHOTE EDITORS

TULA LOTAY VARIANT COVER ARTIST

WELCOME TO THE EXPERIMENT

It started with a conversation between friends.

This one was the old Idris Elba as James Bond debate, and while we didn't add anything new to it, we all realized if there ever *was* a black James Bond, we'd never see what we really wanted: Some huge blockbuster to focus on the unique perspective a black man would have as a British superspy. Because while we believe in "color-blind casting," there's *also* something cool about embracing what a larger-than-life genre looks like from a different perspective.

But what if we imaged a parallel world where that *could* happen? A reality across the horizon where these stories star people from marginalized backgrounds and are unafraid to explore how it makes them unique. What if we *could* smuggle back the pop culture from that world? From that side of the horizon?

What if all it took was just… deciding to do it?

My name is **Pornsak Pichetshote**. I'm a Thai-American former comic book editor who worked for DC's Vertigo imprint and writer of the comic series THE GOOD ASIAN, which won the Eisner and Harvey awards. My first horror book INFIDEL was selected for NPR's 100 Favorite Horror Stories of all Time. Both books succeeded by providing different perspectives on very popular genres, but were still limited by my experience. What if I could open that up?

THE HORIZON EXPERIMENT is me and some of the most talented people I know seeing what's possible. **Five one-shots** co-edited by one of the best editors in comics, Will Dennis, all released monthly and designed to act as pilots for follow-up books if sales merit.

Everyone was given the same challenge: Create a protagonist from a **marginalized background** set in a **popular genre** where if the background of that protagonist changed, so would your story.

The results spanned a range of genres. But while the response to our launch was tremendous, and the reviews were fantastic, we released the books during a very tough market. And yet, even despite this, it was impossible to ignore that the sales for each one-shot increased over the last.

Which brings us to where we are now. Because like it says in the title, this has always been an experiment. And if sales on this collection do well enough, that will give us the confidence to continue some of these series. But which ones? From the start, THE HORIZON EXPERIMENT was designed as a community experience, so we'd love people to get involved and say which series they'd love for us to publish first. And since comic books have a long tradition of being saved by letter-writing campaigns, here's ours: Write in to **thehorizonexperiment@gmail.com** and vote for the one-shots you'd love to have graduate to series the most. Or just scan the QR

THE MANCHURIAN

The first one-shot is mine, and while it's always strange talking about yourself...

Pornsak Pichetshote is a Thai-American who, once upon a time, was a rising-star editor at DC Comics' Vertigo imprint, where he edited such award-winning titles as *Sweet Tooth*, *Daytripper*, and *We3*. He went on to write comics, including the Eisner- and Harvey-winning THE GOOD ASIAN as well as the horror hit INFIDEL. He also writes for television, his credits including *Marvel's Cloak & Dagger* and *Two Sentence Horror Stories*.

OK, I'm much more comfortable talking about superstar artists **Terry** and **Rachel Dodson**. While they've drawn every significant character at Marvel and DC, it's their work on *Spider-Man*, *Harley Quinn*, and *Wonder Woman* that has become iconic. A jack of many trades, Terry's also worked in toy, statue, video game and animation design, art instruction, as well as had gallery exhibitions featuring his paintings. Most recently, his art was the basis for the *DC Heroes United* video game from Genvid Entertainment. Together, the Dodsons co-created the Eisner-nominated series ADVENTUREMAN with award-winning Matt Fraction as well as *The Art of Rachel and Terry Dodson* from Flesk Publications, which is out now.

My go-to letterer and graphic designer **Jeff Powell** has worked on hundreds of comics in his decades-long career in the industry. His work runs the gamut from mainstream favorites like DEADLY CLASS, *Deadpool*, *Sonic the Hedgehog*, and *Teenage Mutant Ninja Turtles* to acclaimed indie darlings *Atomic Robo* and SCALES & SCOUNDRELS, not to mention having designed books, logos, and trade dress for Marvel, Image, Valiant, and more.

TERRY DODSON PENCILS & COLORS
RACHEL DODSON INKS

"THE MANCHURIAN is the next level spy story you've been waiting for. Smart, fun, crisp writing by Pornsak with superb illustrations by the incredible Dodson team… Superb twists when you need them but don't expect them. And a wow finish that makes the ride all worth it."

—JEPH LOEB
(*Batman: Hush*, *Batman: The Long Halloween*)

"Sitting between le Carré and De Palma's spy thrillers, THE MANCHURIAN is a thoroughly modern and personal take on international espionage that reminds us the lies we tell others are nothing compared to the ones we tell ourselves. The next issue can't come soon enough."

—CLIFF CHIANG
(*Catwoman: Lonely City*, PAPER GIRLS)

"I love the idea of THE HORIZON EXPERIMENT and I loved THE MANCHURIAN — gorgeous and glamorous like Bond, heavy and human like le Carré, it's a piece of spy fiction I never knew I needed and am so grateful to Pornsak and Terry and Rachel for making it. Betcha say the same three words I did by the time you get to the last page: I want more."

—MATT FRACTION
(*Hawkeye*, *Invincible Iron Man*)

"THE MANCHURIAN is a fun, smart, beautifully illustrated spy thriller by two of my favourite creators. My only wish is that Pornsak and Terry would turn it into an ongoing so I could keep reading the monthly escapades of Calvin Low!"

—JEFF LEMIRE
(GIDEON FALLS, *Green Arrow*)

"THE MANCHURIAN by Pichetshote/Dodson fulfils the (secret) brief and more. Walks the glamourous-credible spy-fic line, and then zip-lines back down it for kicks. Give me more."

—KIERON GILLEN
(*Young Avengers*, THE WICKED & THE DIVINE)

KEY WEST
DRIPPING WET UNDER THE FLORIDA SUN, IT HITS ME AGAIN--
--HOW DIFFICULT IT IS TO FIND A GOOD MAN.
OR A GOOD WOMAN.
MADISYN BROWN
The Target
GOOD PEOPLE IN GENERAL.
THEY'RE THE WORLD'S MOST ENDANGERED RESOURCE.

HAHA HAHA!
MMMMMM
IN BEIJING, WE'RE TRAINED TO LOOK FOR GOOD PEOPLE.
INDIVIDUALS WITHOUT MONEY PROBLEMS OR EMOTIONAL ISSUES.
THOSE EAGER TO HELP THEIR COUNTRY.
THEY'RE NOT LOOKING FOR REVENGE.
THEY'RE NOT LONELY.
OR HORNY.
PETER BROWN
The Target's Very Annoyed Brother
YES!
AND WHEN YOU KEEP MEETING GOOD PEOPLE, YOU WONDER WHY THE WORLD SEEMS OUT TO HELP EVERYONE ELSE.
WHY CAN'T GOOD THINGS HAPPEN TO GOOD PEOPLE TOO?

PRESIDENT'S YEARS LONG DIPLOMATIC DANCE WITH CHIN

LEAKED FILES REVEAL FINANCIAL NETWORK USING
MERICAN NONPROFITS TO PUSH CHINESE PROPAGAND

WHY A U.S. GENERAL WARNS WAR WITH
HINA POSSIBLE IN LESS THAN FIVE YEARS

from: August.Patel@pythia_consultant.com
date: Wed, Aug 23, 7:50 AM (1 day ago)
subject: Re: Security risks

Mr. Goodman has to understand the differences between Chinese and American spycraft. Firstly, Chinese espionage is corporate espionage – spying not on American governments but corporations – because of (1) China's expanding role as a financial superpower, and (2) that being where a country's true political will lies.

There's actually little overlap between Chinese and Western espionage. For one, the Chinese don't pay for intelligence. They believe people would never knowingly commit espionage but would instead be indiscreet under the right circumstances.

China is not looking to recruit spies as much as "good people" willing to gossip and help China modernize. And with the unfettered travel back and forth into China, these gossips are recruited by China's top spy agency, the **Ministry of State Security (M.S.S.)**, while visiting the country.

Paul Moore, the former senior China analyst for the FBI, uses

US ALLEGES ELITE HACKING TEAMS
BACKED BY CHINA'S GOVERNMENT

HINA CLAIMS OWNERSHIP OF SECOND SPY BALLOO

OW THE US PLANS TO CURB FLOW O
MERICANS' SENSITIVE DATA TO CHI

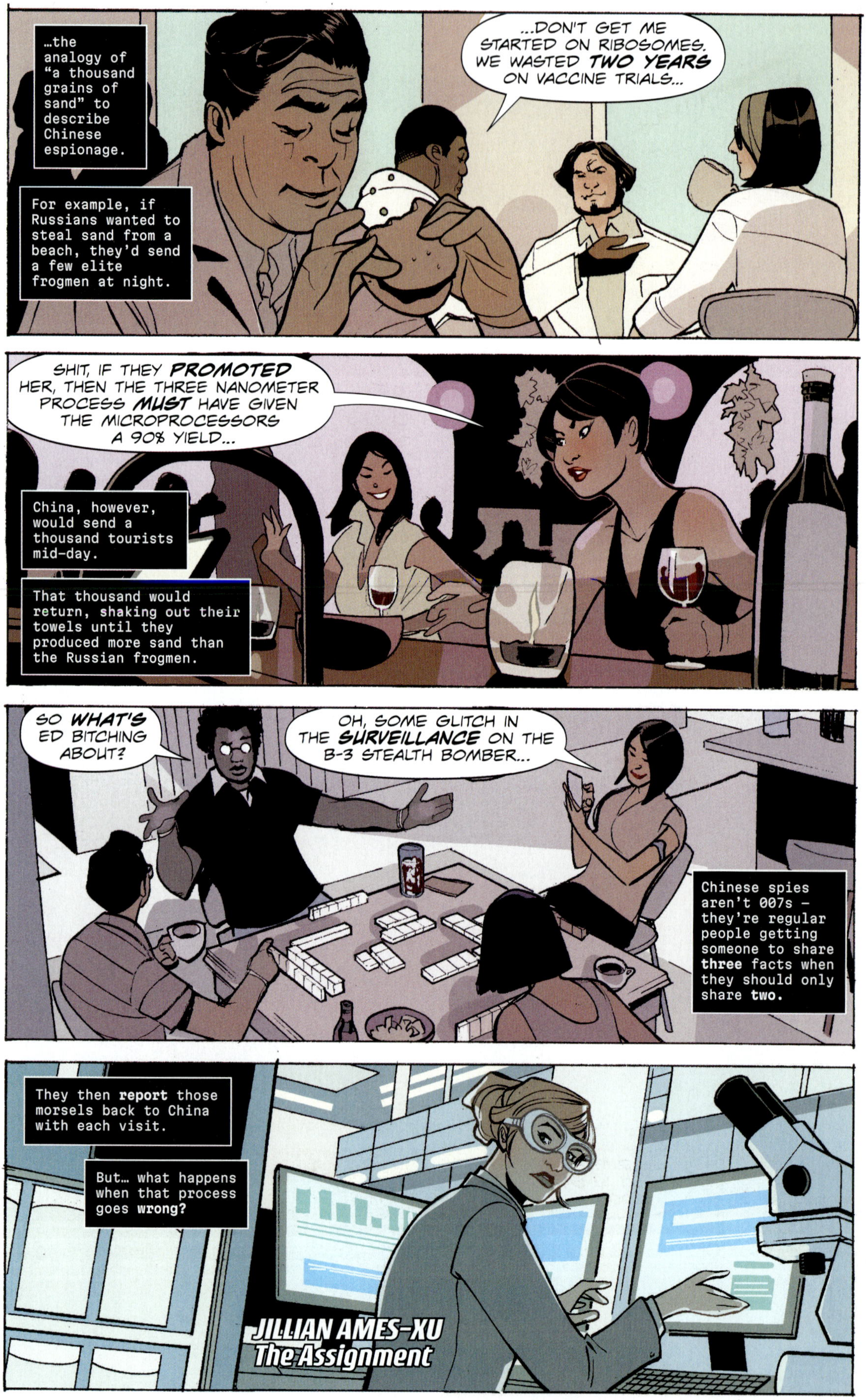

…the analogy of "a thousand grains of sand" to describe Chinese espionage.
For example, if Russians wanted to steal sand from a beach, they'd send a few elite frogmen at night.
...DON'T GET ME STARTED ON RIBOSOMES. WE WASTED **TWO YEARS** ON VACCINE TRIALS...
SHIT, IF THEY **PROMOTED** HER, THEN THE THREE NANOMETER PROCESS **MUST** HAVE GIVEN THE MICROPROCESSORS A 90% YIELD...
China, however, would send a thousand tourists mid-day.
That thousand would return, shaking out their towels until they produced more sand than the Russian frogmen.
SO **WHAT'S** ED BITCHING ABOUT?
OH, SOME GLITCH IN THE **SURVEILLANCE** ON THE B-3 STEALTH BOMBER...
Chinese spies aren't 007s – they're regular people getting someone to share **three** facts when they should only share **two.**
They then **report** those morsels back to China with each visit.
But… what happens when that process goes **wrong?**
JILLIAN AMES-XU
The Assignment

SAN FRANCISCO
I DOWNLOADED A COPY OF THE TARGETING SOFTWARE FOR SWANN'S NEW MILITARY DRONES...
...THEY SPENT TENS OF MILLIONS DEVELOPING IT...
LEWIS EXHIBIT
...AND NOW IT'S OURS.
JILLIAN-- WE DON'T NEED DRONES. WE NEED YOU TO STOP.
SWANN'LL NEVER KNOW--!
THE IDEA IS TO GET GOSSIP-- INFORMATION-- NOT OUTRIGHT STEAL--
A BALLCAP AND A FAKE MUSTACHE LATER, AND I'M MEETING JILLIAN AMES-XU AGAIN. I'VE BEEN ASSIGNED TO PROTECT HER.
YOU'RE ON A LIST OF SUSPECTS SWANN'S INVESTIGATING FOR THEFT.
SHE WORKS FOR SWANN GLOBAL TECHNOLOGIES-- ONE OF AMERICA'S LEADING DEFENSE CONTRACTORS...
WH-- WHAT...?
GOD, THIS EXHIBIT IS SO COOL...
...BUT HER IDEA OF CHINA'S PRIORITIES ARE CONTINUALLY MISGUIDED--THE RELICS OF AN OUTDATED WAR.

SHE'S ALSO BEEN INCREASINGLY CARELESS, AND IF CAUGHT, NOT ONLY WILL SHE BE INVESTIGATED--
THAT-- THAT'S NOT--
SO WILL HER LATE HUSBAND-- AND HIS PEERS.
--POSSIBLE...?
DOZENS OFFERING INTELLIGENCE ABOUT A PROJECT CALLED ADDITIVE X-53--A SYNTHETIC SEED THAT GROWS GRAIN IN ANY CLIMATE.
X-53 WOULD BE WORTH BILLIONS TO A COUNTRY WITH OVER 1.36 BILLION MOUTHS TO FEED LIKE CHINA'S.
BECAUSE IN THE NEW COLD WAR, MONEY IS THE MOST TERRIFYING MUNITION.
WHERE DID YOU...?
LOOK, IT'S--IT'S OK. I KNOW HOW TO GET SECURITY OFF MY--
STOP. I'M BEGGING YOU.
JUST LET YOUR GUARDIAN ANGEL... ANGEL.

WHICH IS WHY IT WAS FINALLY TIME TO PAY A VISIT TO CASPAR CAIN'S LOFTY PENTHOUSE...
CASPAR CAIN
Swann Chief Quality Officer
FUCK THEM. YOU KIDDING?
NOPE. I JUST HEARD.
TEN YEARS, I'VE BEEN THERE, AND FUCKING BARNES GETS SVP?
SWANN THINKS HE'S READY.
HE WAS PITY-PROMOTED 'CUZ HIS BRAT DIED.
TELL ME I'M WRONG.
GOD, I CAN'T FUCKIN' WAIT FOR VERTEX'S PAYOUT TO GO THROUGH. THEN I'LL GET WHAT I REALLY DESERVE.
WHEN JILLIAN LEARNED HER HUSBAND WAS WORKING TO HELP CHINA, SHE WANTED TO JOIN IN. EVEN AFTER HE DIED.
I WAS ASSIGNED TO HER SHORTLY AFTER--BUT THE MORE I'VE URGED HER TO BE CAUTIOUS, THE LESS DISCRETE SHE'S GOTTEN.

BUT THAT'S THE PROBLEM WITH PEOPLE.
THEY'RE UNPREDICTABLE.
BABE, YOU STILL NEVER EMPTIED THE TRASH--
...
IF JILLIAN'S FOUND OUT, IT COULD BRING ATTENTION TO THE LEAKS AROUND X-53--
MAKING HER A PROBLEM THE M.S.S. WANTS PERMANENTLY SOLVED.
CALVIN LOW, AS I LIVE AND BREATHE...
AND HERE I THOUGHT YOU ALREADY SEDUCED ME.
YEAH...I HAD THE TUX ADJUSTED, SO I FIGURED I'D TRY IT OUT.
YOU KNOW, BEFORE WE WERE ALREADY DOWN AT YOUR BESTIE'S WEDD--
MMMMMMM

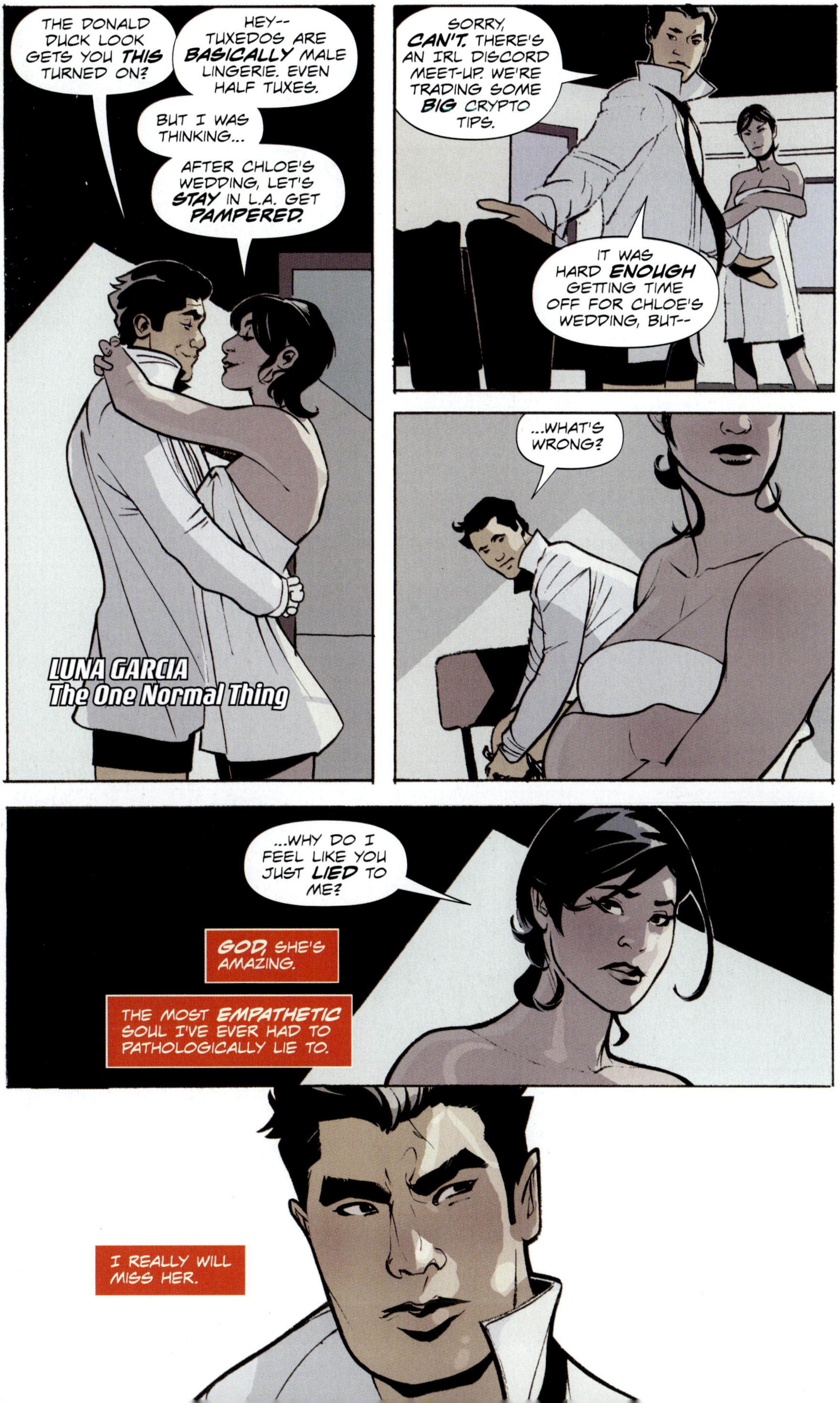
THE DONALD DUCK LOOK GETS YOU THIS TURNED ON?
HEY-- TUXEDOS ARE BASICALLY MALE LINGERIE. EVEN HALF TUXES.
BUT I WAS THINKING...
AFTER CHLOE'S WEDDING, LET'S STAY IN L.A. GET PAMPERED.
LUNA GARCIA
The One Normal Thing
SORRY, CAN'T. THERE'S AN IRL DISCORD MEET-UP. WE'RE TRADING SOME BIG CRYPTO TIPS.
IT WAS HARD ENOUGH GETTING TIME OFF FOR CHLOE'S WEDDING, BUT--
...WHAT'S WRONG?
...WHY DO I FEEL LIKE YOU JUST LIED TO ME?
GOD, SHE'S AMAZING.
THE MOST EMPATHETIC SOUL I'VE EVER HAD TO PATHOLOGICALLY LIE TO.
I REALLY WILL MISS HER.

COME ON. DON'T MAKE THIS AN EMOTIONAL GIRL THING--
EXCUSE ME?
I'M NOT STUPID, YOU KNOW. I CAN TELL WHEN YOU'RE LYING--
CALVIN...?
kreekk
CALVIN!
SHIT. THAT SOUND--!
WHOA, I THOUGHT I CLOSED THAT WINDOW...
SHE DID. BUT THE VISITOR WHO WAS JUST HERE LET ME OVERHEAR HER. WHICH IS HER DISCRETE SIGNAL...

...FOR AN EVEN MORE DISCRETE MEETING.
WOW. SHE'S BEAUTIFUL. CAN I PET HER?
SURE, SHE DOESN'T BITE.
YIP! YIP!
YEAH, THIS DOG IS VERY HAPPY.*
*The situation's being handled.
VIRGINIA "Trouble"
TOO BAD HER OWNER DOESN'T ALWAYS THINK SO.*
*I wouldn't be here if our supervisors agreed.
LIKE ME, VIRGINIA IS A MANSHU--AN AGENT ASSIGNED TO BE GUARDIAN ANGELS FOR CHINESE SPIES.
*The Garden thinks your friend's a mess that needs cleaning.
*If you were sanctioned for that, she'd be dead already.
WE'RE TASKED TO HELP THOSE IN OVER THEIR HEADS--BY ANY MEANS NECESSARY.
SO THOSE SPIES NEVER BREAK THE LAW AND RISK EXPOSURE.
EVERY MANSHU PROTECTS SPIES IN THE CITY THEY'RE STATIONED--
YIP! YIP!

BUT WHEN..."PERSPECTIVE" IS NEEDED, AN OUT-OF-TOWNER IS SENT IN.
CALM DOWN, GIRL...
*You're here to pressure me. Which means the Garden thinks Jillian can turn herself around.
*Or maybe this is where my friend has the best shot.
*Maybe the Garden thinks you're caring about the wrong things now.
*As if you'd resort to anything as blunt as a sniper.
*You know me so well.
*And if you knew me...
*Your bottle wouldn't have been left exposed while you were focused on the dog.
*Let's go then.

YOU THINK I DON'T KNOW WHEN SOMEONE'S BLUFFING?
*What are you--
NO ONE'S IN EARSHOT. WE DON'T NEED THE DAMN CODE.
VIRGINIA, I'LL MAKE JILLIAN LISTEN--
THAT'S NOT YOUR JOB. YOUR JOB IS EXPEDIENCE.
WE WERE CREATED BECAUSE THE WORLD IS EVOLVING--AND OUR SIDE NEEDS PEOPLE TO DO WHAT THEIRS CAN--
NOT AT THE EXPENSE OF WHO WE'RE PROTECTING--
OH, THE M.S.S. HIT THE JACKPOT WITH YOU, HUH?
WILL YOU QUIT YOUR DAMN STRETCH--
CHINESE ENOUGH TO BE A MANSHU. CAUCASIAN ENOUGH TO BE ACCEPTED INTO A COUNTRY FOUNDED UPON WHITE SUPREMACY.
GUILTY ENOUGH TO BE TORTURED BY ALL OF IT.
WE'RE PROOF BOTH SIDES NEED TO EVOLVE.
BECAUSE AT NO OTHER POINT HAS OUR ENEMY BEEN AS DIVIDED AS THEY ARE NOW. ITS PEOPLE AS DISILLUSIONED.
SO DON'T MAKE YOURSELF A PROBLEM TOO.

Many have inquired if there are commonalities linking Chinese spies. But while the country has generally targeted ethnic Chinese for these roles in the past, there is good reason to believe any previous profiles should be broadened.

The world has watched China pull itself from poverty to become a global superpower in the span of a generation. This, even as faith in the United States continues to weaken. Many are willing to chalk up reports of the country's disregard of human rights as Western propaganda to justify currying favor with its multi-billion-dollar economy. In the following series of reports, we detail how there may be more Chinese spies in America than ever. But rather than ethnic Chinese as historically has been the case, these new spies hail from all religions, ethnicities, and races.

Our last section details growing rumors concerning a new thirteenth branch of Chinese espionage – referred to in whispers as "Manshus" – or "Manchurians" as it translates in English. What role do they play, as some experts believe China is becoming more ambitious than ever?

KNOWN BRANCHES OF THE MINISTRY OF STATE SECURITY (M.S.S.)

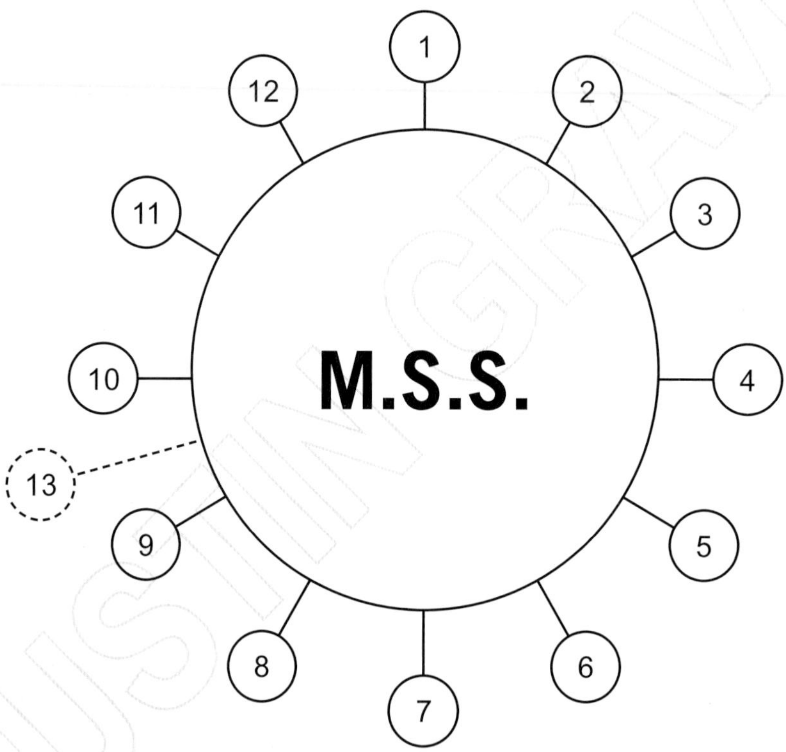

1 – Recruitment
2 – Spy management
3 – Operations in Taiwan, Hong Kong & Macao
4 – Technology
5 – Domestic intelligence
6 – Counterintelligence
7 – Intelligence reports
8 – Research
9 – Countersurveillance
10 – Scientific & technical intelligence
11 – Computers
12 – Foreign affairs
13 – Manshus??

A POST ON A HARRY POTTER REDDIT INNOCENTLY INQURING ABOUT "AVADA KEDAVRA" SPELLS.
JILLIAN'S CODE FOR TROUBLE--
OH MY GOD, PLEASE--
--AND TO MEET AT OUR RENDEZVOUS POINT.
WHO ARE YOU RUNNING FROM?
OH-- OH GOD, IT'S YOU-- I--I--
I TRIED TELLING YOU... I'M OLD FRIENDS WITH SOMEONE ON SWANN'S SECURITY TEAM. HIS NAME'S TRAVIS GRAVES--
HE'S GOT A CRUSH ON ME, OK?
AND HE'S BEEN COMPLAINING ABOUT SWANN--SO I INVITED HIM OUT, THINKING I COULD TURN HIM IF I--I TOLD HIM...
SHIT.

I TELL HER TO STAY HERE. BECAUSE I'VE MEMORIZED EVERYTHING ABOUT SWANN'S SECURITY TEAM...
SORRY. YOU'LL HAVE TO TRY A LITTLE HARDER TO LOSE ME.
TRAVIS?
...SO I KNOW SHE PICKED THE WORST PAIN-IN-THE-ASS TO CONFIDE IN.
TRAVIS-- WAIT!
SO, LIKE YOU WERE SAYING--
TRAVIS GRAVES
Swann Security, Former CIA
TRAVIS GRAVES SERVED TWO TOURS IN AFGHANISTAN BEFORE HE JOINED THE AGENCY--AND ENDED UP LIKE MANY FORMER SPIES TO WORK CORPORATE SECURITY.

OF COURSE, KILLING HIM ISN'T THE PROBLEM.
THE TRICK IS NOT MAKING IT LOOK LIKE A PROFESSIONAL'S WORK.
A MAGAZINE WITH ITS SPINE ROLLED IN HAS THE BLUNT STRENGTH OF A STEEL ROD.
WHICH MEANS, EVEN HIS THICK HEAD WILL CRACK WITH ENOUGH--
UHHH!!

DAMMIT--
HE'S QUICKER THAN I--
DON'T GET FANCY JUST--
BLAM
I TAKE GRAVES' BODY WITH ME. I'LL FIND A MORE THOROUGH WAY TO DISPOSE OF IT LATER.

THAT'S IT... HAND OVER YOUR HEART.
KEEP YOUR EYES CLOSED.
NOW TAKE A FEW MORE... SLOW... BREATHS...
BECAUSE NOW, THE REAL WORK STARTS.
YOU...
...YOU KILLED HIM, DIDN'T YOU?
THAT MEANS YOU KILLED HIM, DIDN'T YOU??
YOU DON'T HAVE TO WORRY ABOUT HIM ANYMORE.
NOW WOULD BE THE MOMENT.
TO TERRIFY HER. MAKE HER FEEL THE DEATHS SHE'LL BE RESPONSIBLE FOR IF SHE DOESN'T STOP.
BUT... WE WERE TAUGHT TO LOOK FOR GOOD PEOPLE.
I'M SORRY I NEVER MET YOUR HUSBAND.
FROM WHAT I GATHER, PEOPLE REALLY LOVED HIM. HE WORKED HIS ASS OFF--
SENDING MONEY BACK TO HIS PARENTS IN SHANDONG--MOVING THEM HERE SO THEY COULD ALL BE CLOSE--
HAVING THEM LIVE IN A COUNTRY THEY WOUND UP HATING.

THEY SOUND EXACTLY LIKE THE TYPE OF PARENTS WHO'D HATE THEIR GOOD CHINESE SON NOT MARRYING A GOOD CHINESE WOMAN.
HE'D HAVE TO BE A VERY GOOD MAN, DEEPLY IN LOVE, TO DO IT ANYWAY.
AND IT TAKES A GOOD WOMAN TO WANT TO PROVE TO HERSELF SHE'S WORTH THAT LOVE.
YOU--YOU DON'T... UNDERSTAND...
LOOK AT ME.
WE ARE THE PEOPLE WE ARE. WE'RE BORN THE WAY WE'RE BORN.
WE JUST HAVE TO FIND A WAY TO LIVE WITH IT.
YOU HAVE TO LET THIS GO.

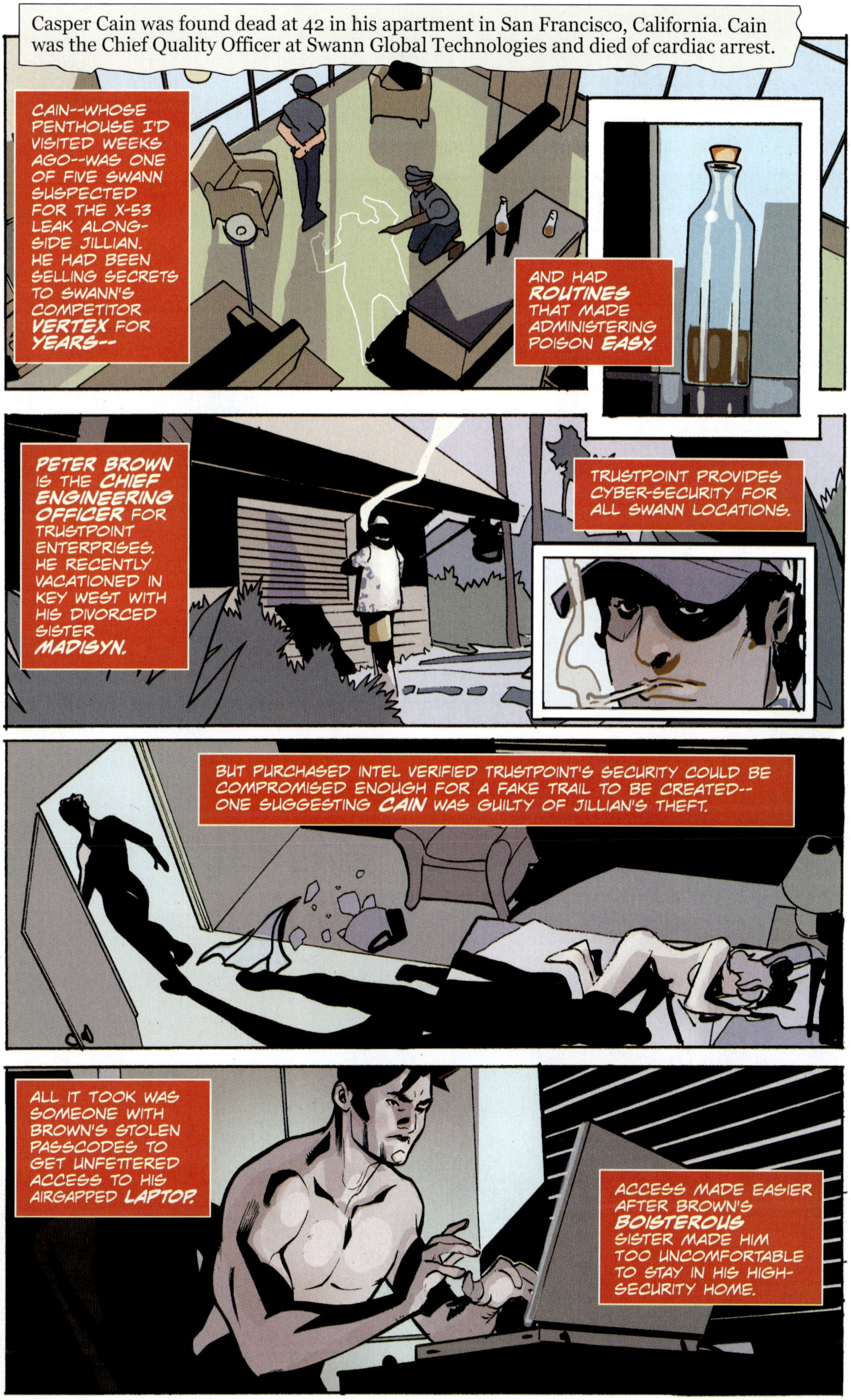
Casper Cain was found dead at 42 in his apartment in San Francisco, California. Cain was the Chief Quality Officer at Swann Global Technologies and died of cardiac arrest.
CAIN--WHOSE PENTHOUSE I'D VISITED WEEKS AGO--WAS ONE OF FIVE SWANN SUSPECTED FOR THE X-53 LEAK ALONGSIDE JILLIAN. HE HAD BEEN SELLING SECRETS TO SWANN'S COMPETITOR VERTEX FOR YEARS--
AND HAD ROUTINES THAT MADE ADMINISTERING POISON EASY.
PETER BROWN IS THE CHIEF ENGINEERING OFFICER FOR TRUSTPOINT ENTERPRISES. HE RECENTLY VACATIONED IN KEY WEST WITH HIS DIVORCED SISTER MADISYN.
TRUSTPOINT PROVIDES CYBER-SECURITY FOR ALL SWANN LOCATIONS.
BUT PURCHASED INTEL VERIFIED TRUSTPOINT'S SECURITY COULD BE COMPROMISED ENOUGH FOR A FAKE TRAIL TO BE CREATED--ONE SUGGESTING CAIN WAS GUILTY OF JILLIAN'S THEFT.
ALL IT TOOK WAS SOMEONE WITH BROWN'S STOLEN PASSCODES TO GET UNFETTERED ACCESS TO HIS AIRGAPPED LAPTOP.
ACCESS MADE EASIER AFTER BROWN'S BOISTEROUS SISTER MADE HIM TOO UNCOMFORTABLE TO STAY IN HIS HIGH-SECURITY HOME.

Casper Cain
5/29/1986 - 9/25/2024
IN THE TWO WEEKS IT'S TAKEN FOR CAIN'S BODY TO BE FOUND--
BEVERLY HILLS
JILLIAN HASN'T TRIED ANYTHING NEW. BUT I'LL KEEP CHECKING IN.
BECAUSE SHE'S A GOOD PERSON. AND GOOD THINGS OUGHT TO HAPPEN TO GOOD PEOPLE.
LIKE LUNA.
WE'LL BREAK UP SOON. AND SHE'LL FIND A DECENT-- HONEST--MAN.
UNTIL THEN...I'VE JUST TRIED TO BE GOOD TO HER. TO BE THE MAN A WOMAN LIKE HER DESERVES.
BECAUSE...GOOD THINGS OUGHT TO HAPPEN TO GOOD PEOPLE.
UGHHH!
NO
NO...
...HAND OVER...

...HEART...
...EYES... CLOSED...
...SLOW... BREATHS...
CALVIN!!
IT'S... I'M...OK...
CALVIN... I SAW THE PAROXETINE IN THE TRASH. IN YOUR BATHROOM THAT MORNING I WAS OVER.
"DOCTORS PRESCRIBE IT FOR PANIC ATTACKS. MY DAD HAD THEM. HE WORKED IN A HIGH-STRESS JOB TOO.
"I MEAN, NOT AS MUCH AS FINANCE, BUT...
LOW, CALVIN
PAROXETINE
10 MG TABLET
TAKE 2 TABLETS
BY MOUTH TWICE
I GREW UP AROUND THIS, SO TRUST ME-- I KNOW--
THEY GET WORSE IF YOU'RE NOT HONEST ABOUT THEM.

I KNOW.
THEY...JUST **STARTED.** OUT OF **NOWHERE**. NOT WHEN THINGS ARE... STRESSFUL, BUT WHEN THEY'RE **CALM.**
IT'S BEEN HAPPENING FOR **MONTHS,** AND I...I DON'T KNOW WHAT'S TRIGGERING THEM.
I JUST...
...I CAN'T GET THEM TO **STOP...**
BUT IF GOOD THINGS HAPPEN TO GOOD PEOPLE, WHAT HAPPENS TO THOSE WHO DO **BAD** FOR THEM?

SAN PAOLO
WHAT DO THEY GET?
AND YOU THINK THEY'RE RESPONSIBLE FOR TRAVIS'S DEATH?
CHINESE SPIES, MR.... PATEL?
I ASSURE YOU. IF WE REGARDED THIS MATTER WITH ANY OF THE INCREDULITY IN YOUR VOICE, I WOULDN'T BE HERE.
YOU KEEP SAYING "WE." WHO'S "WE"?
LET'S JUST SAY... CHINESE ESPIONAGE HAS COST THE TOP FIVE AMERICAN CONGLOMERATES BILLIONS OF DOLLARS...
...AND THEY'RE UNACCUSTOMED TO DISCOMFORT.
SO WHAT? YOUR BILLIONAIRE BOYS' CLUB WANTS TO GO TO WAR?
THAT'S NOT THE IMPORTANT PART, MR. GRAVES.
THE IMPORTANT PART IS WE KNOW YOUR BROTHER, TRAVIS GRAVES, SPENT HIS CAREER AT THE CIA TRYING TO LIVE UP TO YOUR MANY ACCOMPLISHMENTS.
AND MY EMPLOYERS ARE WILLING TO SPEND MILLIONS TO HELP YOU AVENGE HIS MURDER AT THE HANDS OF THESE SPIES.
AUSTIN GRAVES
More Trouble
MAYBE THOSE PEOPLE WHO DO BAD FOR THEM, ALL THEY GET IS THIS...

SAN FRANCISCO
...A MOMENT.
CALVIN-- NO--NO!
I THINK ABOUT WHAT VIRGINIA SAID. ABOUT HOW THE MANSHUS ARE EVOLVING.
WHICH MEANS WE'LL SOON BE ASKED TO DO MORE THAN EVER.
AND WE'LL HAVE TO SACRIFICE.
FINE. I WON'T CHANGE THE CHANNEL, BUT SEE?
BUT UNTIL THEN... A MOMENT'S NOT BAD.
WHO NEEDS L.A. WHEN WE'VE GOT THE FARRELLY BROTHERS?
TO THE RIGHT MAN, A MOMENT CAN MEAN THE WORLD.
A WORLD THAT HAS A PLACE FOR DECENCY-- FOR GOODNESS.
AND THAT HAS TO BE WORTH FIGHTING FOR.
I WARNED YOU...DON'T LET THE GARDEN THINK YOU'RE A PROBLEM...
DOESN'T IT?
END

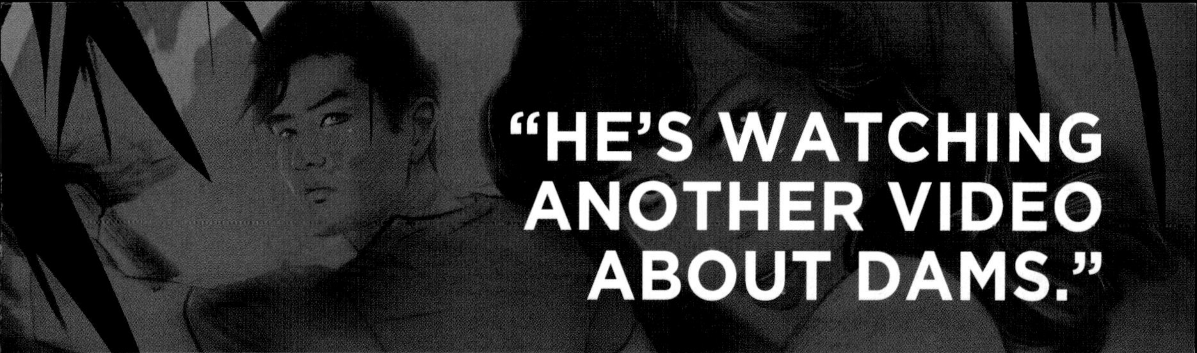

"HE'S WATCHING ANOTHER VIDEO ABOUT DAMS."

In the years leading up to my father's passing, he could always be found in front of a documentary about Chinese dams. To him, they were symbols of Chinese excellence, of the ingenuity it took for a country where over a billion lived in poverty to turn itself into a global superpower in the span of a couple generations. In his latter years, Dad became deeply proud of his Chinese heritage—a culture he barely knew, a language he didn't speak—insisting on family vacations there, telling us at every turn why we should move there.

Of course, I'd talk about its well-documented human rights violations — its stringent censorship and stifling of religious, amongst other, freedoms. He'd counter with America's history of instigating wars in other countries and its constant racial inequalities. And on and on, we'd argue.

THE MANCHURIAN is an ode to my father's China, building on well-documented reports of Chinese espionage (a topic I find fascinating in its contrast to Western spycraft) to create a larger-than-life mythology that, in the end, isn't any more accurate than James Bond's reportage of MI-6, but hopefully just as action-packed and thrilling. Throw in some inspiration from shows like *The Americans* and *The Equalizer*, and you have Calvin Low—a Chinese James Bond acting as a fixer / guardian angel to other spies secretly working in the US, packaged in a series interested in telling stories about American disillusionment. Of all the ways people today can feel betrayed by their countries, communities, and institutions—as well as what they might do in response.

And nowhere is that more apparent than in the complicated, hypocritical figure of Calvin Low himself, who is on a slow exploration to evaluate the depths to which he can lie and rationalize to himself.

When I conceived of the idea, I told my editor and dear friend Will Dennis, that we needed a Terry Dodson-type of artist, and who did we know who could pull that off? Will replied, "Why don't we just ask Terry Dodson?" And that's why Will's one of the best editors in comics.

To say working with Terry and Rachel Dodson is an honor is a supreme understatement. I consider Terry and Rachel comic book royalty, and a look at their credits explains why. While I've been blessed to work with many amazing illustrators, this is the first time where every panel came out exactly as I pictured, just a thousand times more beautiful, and the only explanation I have for that is because I've been a fan of Terry and Rachel for so long that I've grown up thinking in Terry Dodson panels. Combined with my go-to letterer and graphic designer Jeff Powell, Calvin Low is in good hands.

He'll need them as he confronts the conflicts ahead of him: Because how much can he possibly keep doing this before his recently developed panic attacks overwhelm him? But is quitting even an option for him? What happens when he tries? Can he keep his secrets from his beloved Luna? What happens when she discovers the truth? Or is she carrying secrets of her own? Is she as "good" as he thinks? And how long can one man—or even a team of elite men and women—wage war not just against America—but American corporations? And what exactly is the difference?

I hope you can't wait to find out either.

Pornsak Pichetshote

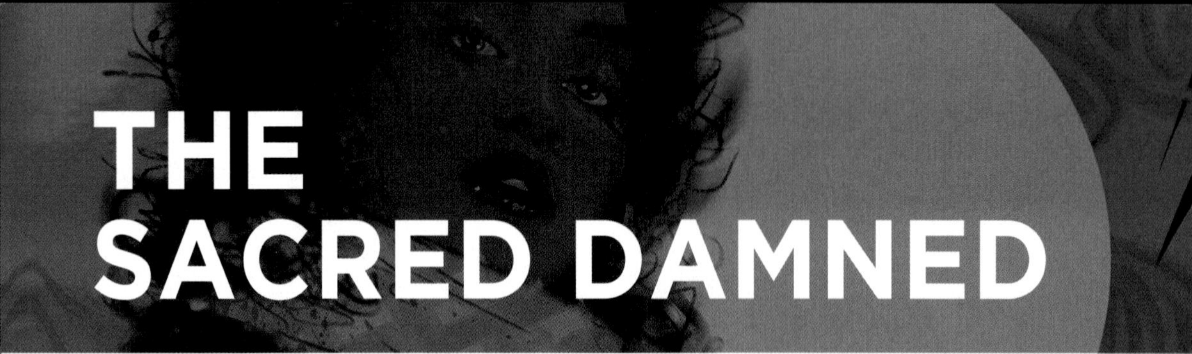

THE SACRED DAMNED

All us geeks are jealous of Pakistani-American writer **Sabir Pirzada**. He's written on some of the most beloved franchises in pop culture, from *Moon Knight* and *Ms. Marvel* for Marvel Studios to *Star Wars: The Bad Batch* for LucasFilm. In comics, he was hand-selected to write the *Ms. Marvel* comic book alongside the MCU's Kamala Khan herself, star Iman Vellani. Not content to rest on his laurels, his first Image graphic novel DANDELION was released in July.

Eisner winner **Michael Walsh** has quickly become one of the pre-eminent voices in comic book horror. He's worked for Marvel, DC, Disney, *Magic: The Gathering* and many others, but is best known as the creator, writer, and artist of the Eisner-nominated horror series THE SILVER COIN and for his YA graphic novel *The Oates & The Elphyne*.

Becca Carey's penchant for the handmade approach has made her a cover artist, letterer, and graphic designer to watch in comics. She has worked at all the major publishers on such hit books as *Wonder Woman*, *Batgirl*, *Batman*, *Buffy the Vampire Slayer*, RADIANT BLACK, and more.

MICHAEL WALSH ART & COLOR

"Terrifyingly gripping and may trigger a curious craving for cookies!"

—IMAN VELLANI (actor/writer, *Ms. Marvel*)

"Eerie, dreary, and makes me think twice about cookies.
Great work by the whole team!"

—W. MAXWELL PRINCE (ICE CREAM MAN, SWAN SONGS)

"THE SACRED DAMNED feels like it was made for me. A modern take on *The X-Files*, about investigating occult occurances throughout the world, with new horrors at every turn and fresh ways to combat them. I think it'll feel like it was made for you too.

—KUMAIL NANJIANI (actor/writer/comedian *The Big Sick*, *Silicon Valley*)

"THE SACRED DAMNED is a devilishly nasty occult classic in the making.

NOW THEY ONLY WORSHIP EACH OTHER.
هل تحب
أن تأخذ
بسكويتة؟

IT'S TIME TO REMIND THEM.
HEY. I THOUGHT I HEARD YOU SPEAKING ARABIC.
WHAT? WHEN?
LAST NIGHT. MY ARABIC'S FADED SINCE I STUDIED ABROAD, BUT IT SOUNDED LIKE YOU WERE ASKING IF I WANTED A COOKIE?
هل تحب أن تأخذ بسكويتة؟
THAT'S WEIRD. I DON'T EVEN SPEAK ARABIC.

YES! KYLE!
WOW. THAT GUY'S GOOD!
COME ON, GRASSMAN!
GO, GO, GO!!
HELLUVA PASS!
FUCK YEAH!
WHAT-- ALREADY?!
SHIT, THERE GOES TWENTY BUCKS!
THIS IS THE ONE I WANT.
OH, YES. HE LOOKS DELICIOUS.
TSSSSSSSSSSSSS
YEEEAOUCH!
TOUCH DOWN
WHAT THE FUCK?

HI KYLE, I'M A SCOUT FOR CLEVELAND. WHILE THE NFL CANNOT IN ANY OFFICIAL CAPACITY MAKE ANY OFFERS TO YOU WHILE YOU'RE STILL AN UNDERGRAD, I JUST WANTED TO INTRODUCE MYSELF--
I DON'T KNOW HOW YOU DO IT, JUGGLING YOUR STUDIES ON TOP OF FOOTBALL, BUT CONSIDER ME IMPRESSED.
KEEP IT UP.
ALLISON, UH, YOU DON'T HAVE TO--
REALLY.
I WANT TO.
GET THIS. JONES HAS BEEN COMPLAINING ABOUT HOW YOUR JERSEY WAS SO HOT TO THE TOUCH, IT GAVE HIM BURN MARKS. WHAT A FAG.
NOW PEOPLE ARE WRITING HEADLINES THAT YOU'RE TOO HOT TO HANDLE!

INCIDENT #1.
183 LBS.
WHA--
HUH?
KYLE, YOU OKAY, MAN? SOUNDS LIKE YOU WERE SPEAKING ARABIC OR SOMETHING.
I--WHAT? I WAS ASLEEP. I DON'T REMEMBER...
YOU WERE, LIKE, SLEEPWALKING BUT EATING?
SLEEP-EATING?
WHOA, MAN.
INCIDENT #4.
191 LBS.
HAAAH... UNH...
SHIT.

YOU'VE GAINED A LITTLE WEIGHT. BODY FAT PERCENTAGE HAS GONE UP, TOO. IT'S NOT A CAUSE FOR CONCERN BUT LET'S COME UP WITH A DIET PLAN--
IT'S NOT MY DIET. IT'S MY SLEEP. I...SOMETHING IS HAPPENING TO ME.
IN TIMES OF STRESS, THE BODY'S METABOLISM SOMETIMES CHANGES--
NO. YOU'RE NOT LISTENING.
INCIDENT #8.
207 LBS.
"I'M EATING IN MY SLEEP.
"I'VE TRIED EVERYTHING. I EVEN HANDCUFFED MYSELF TO THE BED RAILING ONCE.
"IT DIDN'T WORK. SOMEHOW, THE HANDCUFFS MELTED.
211 LBS.
227 LBS.
"I TRIED CAFFEINE TO STAY AWAKE.
256 LBS.
303 LBS.
317 LBS.
"THEN I TRIED SLEEPING PILLS TO SLEEP MORE DEEPLY.
"NOTHING-- NOTHING SEEMS TO WORK."

INCIDENT #33.
333 LBS.
P'TOO--
OH, NO. NONONO NO--
ALLISON?! ALLISON, WAKE UP!

"I'M TELLING YOU, HE WASN'T CONSCIOUS.
HE'D BEEN TALKING IN HIS SLEEP. EATING IN HIS SLEEP. HE WAS **NOT AWARE** OF WHAT HE WAS DOING UNTIL HE'D WAKE UP.
HE'S A GOOD KID. PERFECT ATTENDANCE RECORD. I DON'T BELIEVE HE'D **WILLINGLY** DO SOMETHING LIKE THIS.
HE HAD COMPLAINED OF SLEEPWALKING INCIDENTS. WE PRESCRIBED A FEW THINGS, AND MY UNDERSTANDING IS THAT HE TOOK THEM REGULARLY. BUT NOTHING HELPED.
IT IS MY MEDICAL OPINION THAT KYLE GRASSMAN **DOES NOT** BELONG IN A PRISON, BUT IN A HOSPITAL.
YOU'RE LOOKING GOOD, KYLE.
I'M STILL SLEEPWALKING. BUT MY BODY CAN NO LONGER FIND SOMETHING TO EAT IN HERE. IT'S THE ONLY REASON I'VE LOST FIVE POUNDS.
WELL, I KNOW SOMEONE WHO MIGHT BE ABLE TO HELP YOU WITH YOUR SITUATION.
WHAT, LIKE A SLEEP SPECIALIST?
NOT EXACTLY.

MEET DR. INAYAH JIBRIL. PROFESSOR OF ETHNOGRAPHY AND THE OCCULT.
I'D SAY IT'S NICE TO MEET YOU, KYLE, BUT WE ALL KNOW THIS ISN'T A HAPPY VISIT. TELL ME, HAVE YOU HEARD OF DJINN?
I ONLY ASK BECAUSE IT'S PLAINLY OBVIOUS TO ME THAT YOU ARE POSSESSED BY ONE.

File Name: OCCULTMATTERSPOD_EP11_DRIJ.mp3

Bill White (Host)
Dr. Inayah Jibril (Guest)

[00:00:00]

BW: With me today on the subject of Djinn is Dr. Inayah Jibril, professor of Ethnography and the Occult. Let's start with the basics. What exactly are Djinn?

[00:00:09]

IJ: In Islamic texts, Djinn are referred to as creatures made of fire, as opposed to humans, who are made of clay. In other words, we're made of different stuff than they are, which is why we don't see them or interact with them unless they want us to. The most famous Djinn in Islamic lore is Satan himself.

In western culture, it would probably be the genie from Aladdin. But it's important to note that this is by no means simply just a "Muslim" concept. Reports of Djinn predate Islam itself.

[00:00:23]

BW: And there are even some Muslim countries that recognize possession by Djinn as a kind of mental illness, is that correct?

[00:00:35]

IJ: Oh, yes. Instances where a guy spontaneously murders his children, for example -- the court systems recognize this and factor it into guilt and sentencing.

[00:00:47]

BW: Do we know what they look or sound like?

[00:00:50]

IJ: It depends on the type of Djinn. There are Ghul, Marid, Ifrit, and others, so it's very hard to narrow down a description, especially since some of them can disguise themselves in the forms of animals we know, like a dog, or a snake. They live much longer than we do, and have their own communities.

[00:01:01]

BW: Have you encountered one yourself?

[00:01:05]

IJ: If I had, and I somehow lived through that ordeal, I wouldn't be so eager to talk about it. 95% of Djinn reports contain human injury or death.

Mama doesnt beleev me.
I told her the jin are reel.
The snake plays hid n seek
with me sometimes.
Hes so funee.
But he told me he
likes my sister more.
That made me sad.

INCIDENT #34.
NOW THAT WE'RE NICE AND TOASTED, ARE YOU GONNA FINALLY TELL ME WHAT WE'RE DOING HERE?
DJINN ARE CREATURES MADE FROM FIRE. CONSEQUENTLY, IT'S FIRELIGHT THAT HELPS REVEAL THEM.
I WOKE UP IN THESE WOODS A FEW TIMES. I'D EATEN A DEER. THEN I'D GET THESE PAINFUL STOMACHACHES. COULDN'T PRACTICE, COULDN'T STUDY.
IT WASN'T JUST THE WEIGHT GAIN THAT RUINED EVERYTHING, YOU KNOW.
OH, CRY ME A RIVER.
EXCUSE ME?
YOU'RE ALIVE. YOU CAN WALK, YOU CAN TALK. YOU'RE STILL YOUNG. IF YOU LIVE THROUGH THIS, YOU CAN DO ANYTHING YOU WANT.
WHAT THE HELL ARE YOU TALKING ABOUT? SIX MONTHS AGO, I HAD A FUTURE IN PRO FOOTBALL! NOW, I'M LIVING IN A MENTAL HOSPITAL. MY GIRLFRIEND IS DEAD. AND I CAN BARELY FIT THROUGH THE FUCKING DOOR.

AND HERE YOU ARE, THROWING YOURSELF A PITY PARTY. YOU WANNA FAT SHAME YOURSELF, GO RIGHT AHEAD. BUT I'M NOT GONNA HELP YOU.
YOU'RE A REAL BITCH, YOU KNOW THAT?
I'D STAY CLOSE TO THE FIRE. THE DJINN LIVE IN THE SHADE OF TREES. IT'S ONE OF THE PLACES WHERE THEY'RE THE STRONGEST.
SNAP
THERE. PROBLEM SOLVED. NOW THE ARAB GHOST CAN GO BACK TO THE FUCKING DESERT WHERE IT CAME FROM!
WHAT MAKES YOU THINK IT'S ARAB?
BECAUSE... BECAUSE I THINK I MET IT FIFTEEN YEARS AGO.

I HAD A WEIGHT PROBLEM WHEN I WAS A KID. ONE TIME, MY MOM BAKED SOME COOKIES, BUT I WASN'T ALLOWED TO EAT ANY UNTIL AFTER DINNER. SO I LOCKED MYSELF IN MY ROOM TO TRY TO HAVE SOME SELF-CONTROL.
THEN COMES THIS THING. FROM UNDER MY BLANKET. AND IT OFFERS ME A COOKIE. I DUNNO, IT SOUNDED LIKE IT WAS SPEAKING ARABIC. BUT, SOMEHOW, I COULD UNDERSTAND IT.
I THOUGHT IT WAS A DREAM, UNTIL...
WHAT...YOU DID SOMETHING...
FWUMP
AND I THOUGHT YOU'D NEVER STOP TALKING.
KYLE, THERE ARE A LOT OF MUSLIMS WHO DRINK ALCOHOL, BUT I'M NOT ONE OF THEM. THIS HERE'S JUST A ROOT BEER. AS FOR YOUR BOTTLE? THAT'S SOMETHING ELSE ENTIRELY.

SORRY IF I MISLED YOU. BUT IF YOU THOUGHT I WAS SOME KIND OF "PROTECTOR OF MANKIND FROM EVIL DEMONS," THEN I'M AFRAID YOU'RE A LITTLE MIXED UP.
YOU SEE, I DON'T THINK THE DJINN ARE ALL THAT BAD. IT TOOK ME A WHILE TO SEE IT, BUT WE HUMANS ARE SO MUCH **WORSE.**
TAKE **YOU,** FOR EXAMPLE. YOU CHEATED ON YOUR MIDTERM EXAMS. AND YOU'RE MORE UPSET ABOUT YOUR **FOOTBALL DREAMS** BEING DASHED THAN THE FACT THAT YOUR EX-GIRLFRIEND IS **DEAD.**
DON'T LOOK SO SURPRISED, KYLE. JUST BECAUSE WE CAN'T SEE THE DJINN DOESN'T MEAN THEY CAN'T SEE **US.**
BUT YOU ALREADY **KNEW** THAT. YOU EVEN TOOK A COOKIE FROM ONE.
THEY'VE BEEN WATCHING YOU FOR A LONG, LONG TIME, KYLE. AND THEY ARE **NOT** IMPRESSED.
IT WASN'T UNTIL YOU STARTED TAKING **SPEED** AND **PCP** THAT THE DJINN FOUND A WAY INTO YOUR MIND. ONCE YOU OPENED THE DOOR, IT SIMPLY HAD TO **WALK** IN.
AND IT'S BEEN FATTENING YOU UP EVER SINCE. WHILE YOU'VE BEEN EATING EVERYTHING ELSE... THE DJINN HAVE BEEN PREPARING TO EAT **YOU.**
NOW...

...WHO'S HUNGRY?

YOU BETTER BE HUNGRY.
HAAAH--
OH, GOD--
IT TOOK ME FIFTEEN YEARS TO PREPARE THIS MEAL FOR YOU, MY BROTHERS AND SISTERS.
AAAUGH!
THAT MAY NOT FEEL LIKE A LONG TIME TO YOU, BUT TRUST ME, IN THIS HIDEOUS SACK OF MEAT?
I CAN'T WAIT TO GET--
SLRP
OUT?
OOPS.

NOW LISTEN UP, ALL OF YOU! THE DRUG I USED ON KYLE'S BODY IS KEEPING YOUR IFRIT FRIEND INSIDE HIM. SO IF YOU'RE PLANNING TO EAT THIS YOUNG MAN...YOU'RE GOING TO HAVE TO EAT YOUR FRIEND, TOO.
WHAT? NO TAKERS?
WHY IS THAT? IS IT BECAUSE YOU VALUE THE LIFE OF YOUR FRIEND? WELL, THIS HUMAN LIFE IS VALUABLE, TOO.
YOU SHOULDN'T HAVE DONE THAT. YOU SEE, WE ARE VERY HUNGRY. AND IF WE CANNOT EAT THIS MEAL...
WE WILL HAVE TO EAT SOMETHING ELSE.
YOU FORGET YOUR PLACE, DJINN.

CREATURES MADE FROM FIRE...
...AND YET YOU FEAR IT JUST AS WE DO.
KASH!
AH!
THAK
FSHK!
KRNCH

WUMP!
WUMP WUMP WUMP
YOU ALL SHOULD HAVE PAID MORE ATTENTION WHEN YOU ENTERED THE CLEARING.
I CREATED AN **ENCLOSURE.** YOU'RE STUCK THERE NOW.
YOU GHULS ARE ONLY SUPPOSED TO EAT DEAD FLESH. BUT YOU'VE GRADUATED TO **LIVE BODIES.** I COULDN'T JUST LOOK THE OTHER WAY AND LET YOU ROAM AROUND FREELY.
HUNH-- WHAT--
I PLAYED THE LONG GAME, KYLE. YOU WERE THE **BAIT.**
WHAT THE FUCK...
NOW, YOU NEED TO GET YOUR ASS **ACROSS** THIS BARRIER IF YOU WANT TO GET RID OF THE DJINN POSSESSING **YOU!**
NNFF...
UH...

I...
I...
WHUMP
KYLE. GET UP.

IN MY PRIME, I BET I'D HAVE BEEN ABLE TO CLIMB UP THIS TREE IN 1.5 SECONDS.
I JUST...
...WHAT'S THE POINT?
I KNOW HOW YOU FEEL. LIKE THERE IS NO WAY TO REBUILD YOUR LIFE. IT'S TRUE, THERE'S NO GOING BACK TO WHAT IT WAS. BUT YOU CAN BUILD A NEW NORMAL.
I... I JUST...
...I DON'T WANT A NEW NORMAL.
OKAY, KYLE. OKAY.

YOU SAID FIRE HURTS THEM? THEN I'LL AT LEAST TAKE ONE OF THEM WITH ME.
AAAAAAUGH!
OOOOH, STOP! HELP ME! HELP!
HAAAAUUGH--

YOU WERE SUPPOSED TO HELP HIM LIVE, NOT GIVE HIM SUICIDAL AFFIRMATION.
OR DO YOU THINK KYLE CHOSE WISELY? BECAUSE YOU WISH YOU'D TAKEN YOUR OWN LIFE WHEN YOU FIRST MET ME?
THIS WAS YOUR DOING, WASN'T IT? YOU GAVE THEM THE IDEA TO EAT A LIVE HUMAN.
YESSSS.
WHY? I KNOW IT WAS FUN FOR YOU, CAUSING CHAOS. BUT HOW DID YOU CONVINCE SO MANY OF THEM TO GO ALONG WITH THIS?
OOOH, IT'S NOT JUST THEM. ALL THE DJINN ARE RILED UP.
WE LIVE SEVEN TIMES LONGER THAN YOU HUMANS. OF COURSE WE NOTICED THAT YOU'RE DESTROYING THE PLANET. WE RELY ON THE SAME TREES YOU DO. THE SAME EARTH. AND YOU'RE KILLING ALL OF IT.
SO WE DECIDED TO STRIKE BACK. STARTING WITH YOUR IDOLS. THE ICONS. IN THIS CASE, A SPORTS STAR. HE'S NOT THE FIRST. AND THERE WILL BE MORE.
ESPECIALLY WHEN JANN IBN JANN ARRIVES.
LIES. THE DJINN LORD IS DEAD.
THE SHIVER IN YOUR SPINE TELLS ME YOU DON'T REALLY BELIEVE THAT, MY DEAR.
BUT IF YOU INSIST YOU'RE JUST COLD, I CAN WARM YOU UP--

ENOUGH. YOU BASTARD-- YOU WANNA PLAY GAMES WITH THE WORLD? YOU GO AHEAD. BUT DON'T PLAY GAMES WITH ME.
WHY NOT? YOU USED TO LOVE PLAYING GAMES WITH ME WHEN YOU WERE A CHILD.
DON'T TELL ME YOU'RE STILL SORE THAT YOU LOST--
GIVE ME BACK MY SISTER!
NEVER.
END.

I'LL BE THE FIRST TO ADMIT THAT I AM A BELIEVER IN THE SUPERNATURAL.

As a practicing Muslim, I find that pill rather easy to swallow. The Quran presents past events in which miracles occurred as fact. It also explicitly states that its intended readership isn't just mankind, but includes Djinn—implying that these supernatural creatures need moral instruction, lest they stray and meddle in our human affairs. It doesn't stop with Djinn—among the final chapters of the Quran are prayers to defend against the evil eye and witchcraft.

Belief in the supernatural is commonplace across much of the Muslim world. It's woven into the fabric of court systems in the Middle East, when, say, an upstanding citizen spontaneously murders his family. Mental health and Djinn possession are both considered, sometimes with equal weight, as guilt and sentencing are determined. Recently, there was an incident in a Malaysian school, in which a class of students claims to have encountered a dark figure after some ancient trees nearby were cut down. Perhaps a Djinn nearby used to live in those trees. Or, perhaps, the students were simply stressed and fell into a collective hysteria.

Here's the kicker: practicing the arts of communing with the supernatural are highly discouraged—some say forbidden—in Muslim circles. Backstreet exorcists and shamans are shunned not just by the secular world, but by fellow Muslims who consider them fringe vigilantes. It's a no-win scenario for such practitioners, where their societies all agree that supernatural evil may rear its ugly head, but actually engaging with it is sacrilegious. The typical hero of a Western horror story is, by default, the villain in an Islamic one.

Despite how widespread such beliefs are across the world, they're rarely represented in fiction. While I love classic horror like *The Exorcist* and Bram Stoker's *Dracula* dearly, I always saw them and their Christian iconography as the starting point to a much larger world—one that includes Islamic lore and many others—where the scares offer an "equal mayhem" opportunity, almost as if the horrors were a reflection of the entire world's fears, not just the Western lens.

If we were going to make a deafening entrance to the crowded horror genre, we'd need an artist whose talent and credibility would be respected by all—and then we'd need to exceed the lofty expectations of that artist's fans. Michael Walsh stepped into the role without so much as a blink. From the earliest layouts to the final color tones, Michael demonstrated his mastery not just of the horror genre (which has been well documented through his gorgeously grisly series THE SILVER COIN), but of the comics medium as a whole, expertly coordinating with Becca Carey's crafty lettering so that every tool at their disposal would be a storytelling device that accentuated the scares. I was starstruck to have Will Dennis, an editor I've long admired, to help assemble such a team and shepherd this comic to its full potential. This was also my first creative partnership with long-time friend Pornsak Pichetshote, whose guidance in my comics career has been so invaluable I'm confident I would not have one without him.

You've just stepped into a dark and dangerous world, one that embraces the long shadows of all cultures' fears. We've only scratched the surface of what lies ahead for Inayah Jibril. The door continues to creak open with frightening possibility. Until we know what lurks beyond, I advise caution when hearing the soft whistles of rustling tree branches in the night.

Sabir Pirzada

MOON DOGS

It's an honor to introduce **Tananarive Due**. The Octavia Butler of horror, she's been a leading voice in Black speculative fiction for more than twenty years, winning the American Book Award for her novel *The Living Blood*. She's also won an NAACP Image Award, a World Fantasy Award, a British Fantasy Award, as well as having her writing included in multiple best-of-the-year anthologies. In TV, she's an executive producer on the groundbreaking documentary *Horror Noire: A History of Black Horror*. Her latest novel *The Reformatory* just won the LA Times Science Fiction, Fantasy & Speculative Fiction Book Prize, earning praise from no less than Stephen King. And while she co-authored the graphic novel *The Keeper* with her husband/collaborator, Steven Barnes, MOON DOGS marks her first solo full-length writing endeavor in comics.

Illustrator **Kelsey Ramsay** exploded on the comics scene with works featured in *Joan Jett and The Black Hearts 40 x 40: I Love Rock n' Roll* and *FAB Breakout Book 1: Mad World*. She's become one of the most consistently sought after artists in comics ever since, illustrating *Dark Spaces: Good Deeds*, part of IDW's Dark Spaces imprint curated by comics superstar, Scott Snyder.

Harvey Award winner **José Villarrubia** is one of the most respected colorists in comics. In his prolific twenty-five-year career, he's often collaborated with artists Jeff Lemire (*Sweet Tooth*), Paul Pope (*Batman: Year 100*), Jae Lee (*Fantastic Four: 1234*), and Richard Corben (*Cage*). As an illustrator and photographer, he's also worked with Alan Moore on *Voice of the*

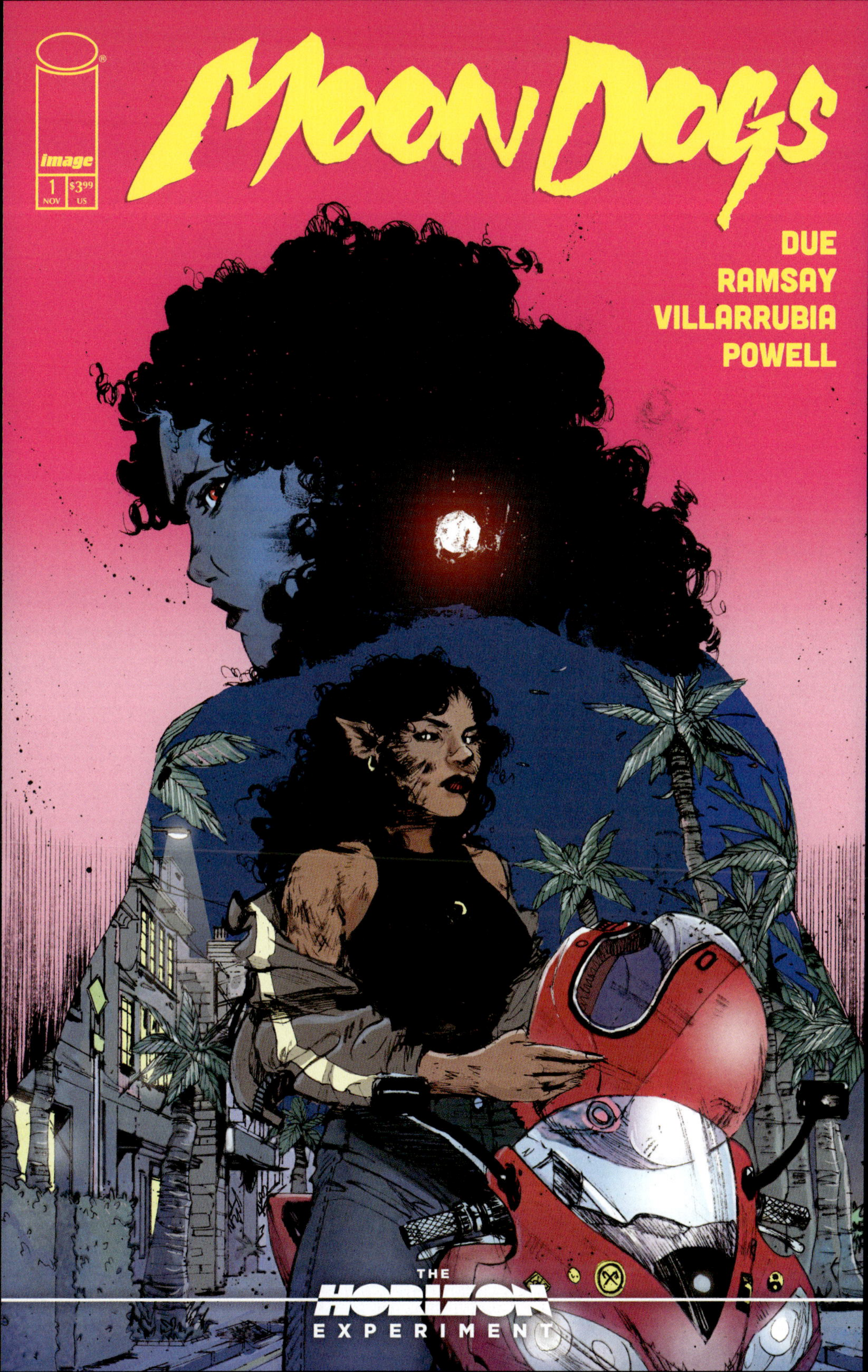

KELSEY RAMSAY ART
JOSÉ VILLARRUBIA COLORS

"I'm a long-time fan of Tananarive Due's work. So much so that I've read every novel and short story she's written. MOON DOGS ranks up at the very top of her work which is saying a lot! It's horror at its finest! Scary in all the right places with characters that make you think and feel. I love this!!"

—RODNEY BARNES
(Peabody-winning writer of KILLADELPHIA and *Winning Time: The Rise of the Lakers Dynasty*).

"Both insightful and entertaining, making it standout as a unique blend of horror and profound social commentary. Tananarive Due brilliantly captures the feeling of otherness through her narrative while Kelsey Ramsay brings this evocative tale to life... truly unique and profound."

—JUSTIN SODERBERG, *Capes & Tights*

"A whip-smart Werewolf take told against the burning heat of Miami, and I love Kelsey Ramsay's art! Evocative and hits the target... MOON DOGS cuts deep."

—JOCK
(WYTCHES, *Batman*)

"Both intellectually stimulating and thrilling, marking it as a standout blend of horror and profound social insight."

—HANK REA, *Lotusland Comics*

"The art in this book is phenomenal. Kelsey Ramsay does a great job of bringing the world to life...The character designs are beautiful and the background art is stunning."

—RICHARD CORYELL, *Nerd Intiative*

LITTLE HAVANA, MIAMI
CARLOS AND I WERE HEADED TO MY HOUSE FOR DINNER WITH MY PARENTS.
IT WAS HARD ENOUGH TO TELL HIM WHO WE REALLY ARE... BUT HE WAS ABOUT TO SEE THE TRUTH UP CLOSE.
THEN WE GOT THE TIP.
THOUGHTS AND PRAYERS TO MY APPETITE. FOR THE REST OF MY LIFE.
I THOUGHT THE PAW PRINT WAS A TRICK OF THE DYING LIGHT.

MOON DOGS?
IT'S NOT CUJO.
BUT...THAT'S... WAIT. IT'S NOT EVEN DARK YET. IT'S NOT EVEN A MOON NIGHT. RIGHT...?
FROM BAD TO WORSE. MUCH WORSE.
NALA! ISN'T THAT...?
I WISH IT WEREN'T, CARLOS.
THIS HAD ALL THE MARKINGS OF WAR.
AND A WAR ABOUT TO TO COME TO MY FRONT DOOR.

STAY AWAY FROM MY SCENE! BACK OFF!
I NEEDED TO TRACK DOWN THIS FERAL BEFORE THE COPS DID.
I WIPED AWAY THE PRINT, BUT LUIS ISN'T STUPID.
DIOS MIO, WHAT HUMAN BEING WOULD DO THIS?
YOU HELP US, WE'LL HELP YOU. THAT'S WHAT MAKES THIS RELATIONSHIP WORK.
THIS ISN'T A "RELATIONSHIP." YOU'RE REPORTERS, I'M POLICE. PERIOD.
MEANING...I'M GOING TO PRETEND I NEVER HAD ANYTHING TO DO WITH YOU AND "YOUR KIND"...IN CASE THIS BLOWS THE CITY WIDE OPEN.
CARNICERIA
I EXPECTED MORE FROM MY OLD FRESHMAN BOYFRIEND AT U.M. THE FIRST BOY I TOLD MY SECRET TO.
NO MORE SPECIAL PRIVILEGES. NO MORE "SECRETS." I'M UP FOR CAPTAIN. HAVE TO BE MORE CAREFUL ABOUT THE COMPANY I KEEP.
TIME FOR YOU TO DISAPPEAR. I'VE GOT NO COMMENT-- AND MONSTERS TO CATCH.
YOU NEED US NOW MORE THAN EVER, LUIS.
AND TRUST ME, WHEN WE CATCH THIS PACK...AND WHEN WE BLOW THEIR HEADS OFF...IT'S BETTER THAN THEY DESERVE.
NOT THE BEST TIME FOR ME TO INTRODUCE CARLOS TO MY WORLD...

Dear Carlos,

You called me out and you're right. I AM afraid to commit. There. You happy now?.

My biggest fear is that one day our differences will come between us. Too many people are learning that my kind exist, and we are tired of hiding.

. You are the most amazing person I've ever met. But you know why my family is different. And I know it hurts your feelings when we seem to be keeping secrets, but our secret has been our protection from the beginning of time.

Believe me, the people who grew up feeling sorry for Lon Chaney, Jr. in those old Universal flicks do NOT feel sorry for real-life lycanthropes.

The people who know are scared, Carlos. You know that. And the more people who know we're here and not just some urban legend, the worse that fear will be.

I know you understand how hard it is just to be Black—but a lycanthrope too? And we've got Mom's genes in the . recipe?

Everyone will be afraid of us. Then it's hunting season on us. So maybe it's up to me and my family to stop ferals before they can start a war.

Because I'm worried about what happens when they're afraid of our child too. (I know, but there's always a small chance!)

I'm tripping. Getting wayyyy ahead of myself, but I wanted to be honest about my thoughts. You deserve that.

So when you say "Let's talk about the future..."

It's a lot to think about.

—Nala

I HAD A FEW QUESTIONS FOR MY BROTHER ABOUT WHAT I'D JUST FOUND. BUT THEY WOULD HAVE TO WAIT.
CAN I TRY THE TEA TOO, MRS. WASHINGTON?
TRUST ME...YOU WOULD NOT LIKE THE TASTE.
BARELY ENOUGH FOR FAMILY, CARLOS. MOON NIGHT'S COMING. THIS IS MY GRANDMOTHER'S BLEND: XABAG HADI AND DINSI. I'M RUNNING VERY LOW.
IT'S NOT FOR HIM ANYWAY.
HEY. NO REASON TO BE RUDE. HE KNOWS WE'RE MOON DOGS.
IT'S FINE. I GET IT. I'M NOT FAMILY.
IT'S NOT FINE, ACTUALLY.
IF YOU DON'T MIND MY ASKING, MR. AND MRS. WASHINGTON... WHAT'S THE TEA FOR? WHY MOON NIGHTS?

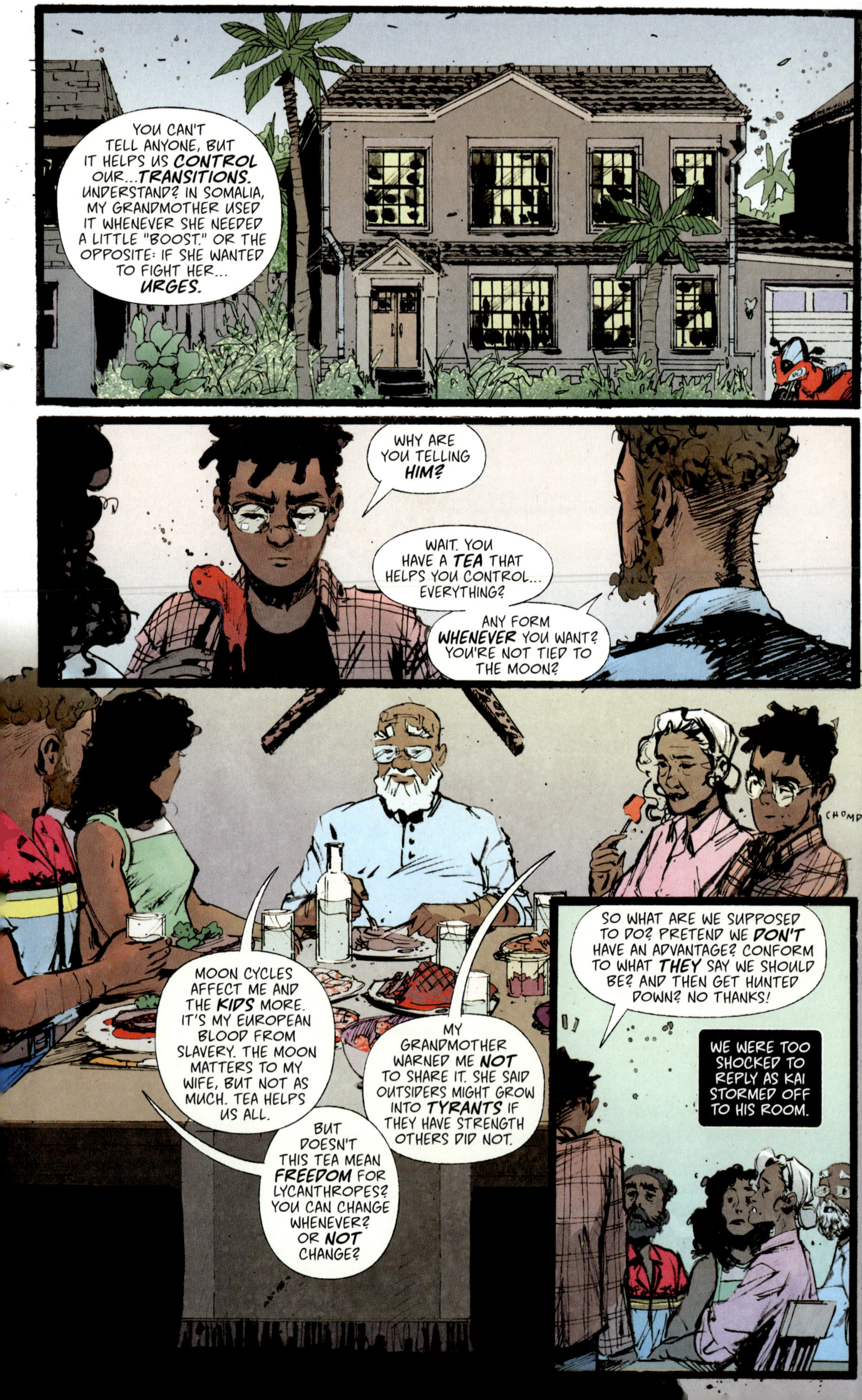
YOU CAN'T TELL ANYONE, BUT IT HELPS US **CONTROL** OUR...**TRANSITIONS.** UNDERSTAND? IN SOMALIA, MY GRANDMOTHER USED IT WHENEVER SHE NEEDED A LITTLE "BOOST." OR THE OPPOSITE: IF SHE WANTED TO FIGHT HER... **URGES.**
WHY ARE YOU TELLING **HIM?**
WAIT. YOU HAVE A **TEA** THAT HELPS YOU CONTROL... EVERYTHING?
ANY FORM **WHENEVER** YOU WANT? YOU'RE NOT TIED TO THE MOON?
CHOMP
MOON CYCLES AFFECT ME AND THE **KIDS** MORE. IT'S MY EUROPEAN BLOOD FROM SLAVERY. THE MOON MATTERS TO MY WIFE, BUT NOT AS MUCH. TEA HELPS US ALL.
MY GRANDMOTHER WARNED ME **NOT** TO SHARE IT. SHE SAID OUTSIDERS MIGHT GROW INTO **TYRANTS** IF THEY HAVE STRENGTH OTHERS DID NOT.
BUT DOESN'T THIS TEA MEAN **FREEDOM** FOR LYCANTHROPES? YOU CAN CHANGE WHENEVER? OR **NOT** CHANGE?
SO WHAT ARE WE SUPPOSED TO DO? PRETEND WE **DON'T** HAVE AN ADVANTAGE? CONFORM TO WHAT **THEY** SAY WE SHOULD BE? AND THEN GET HUNTED DOWN? NO THANKS!
WE WERE TOO SHOCKED TO REPLY AS KAI STORMED OFF TO HIS ROOM.

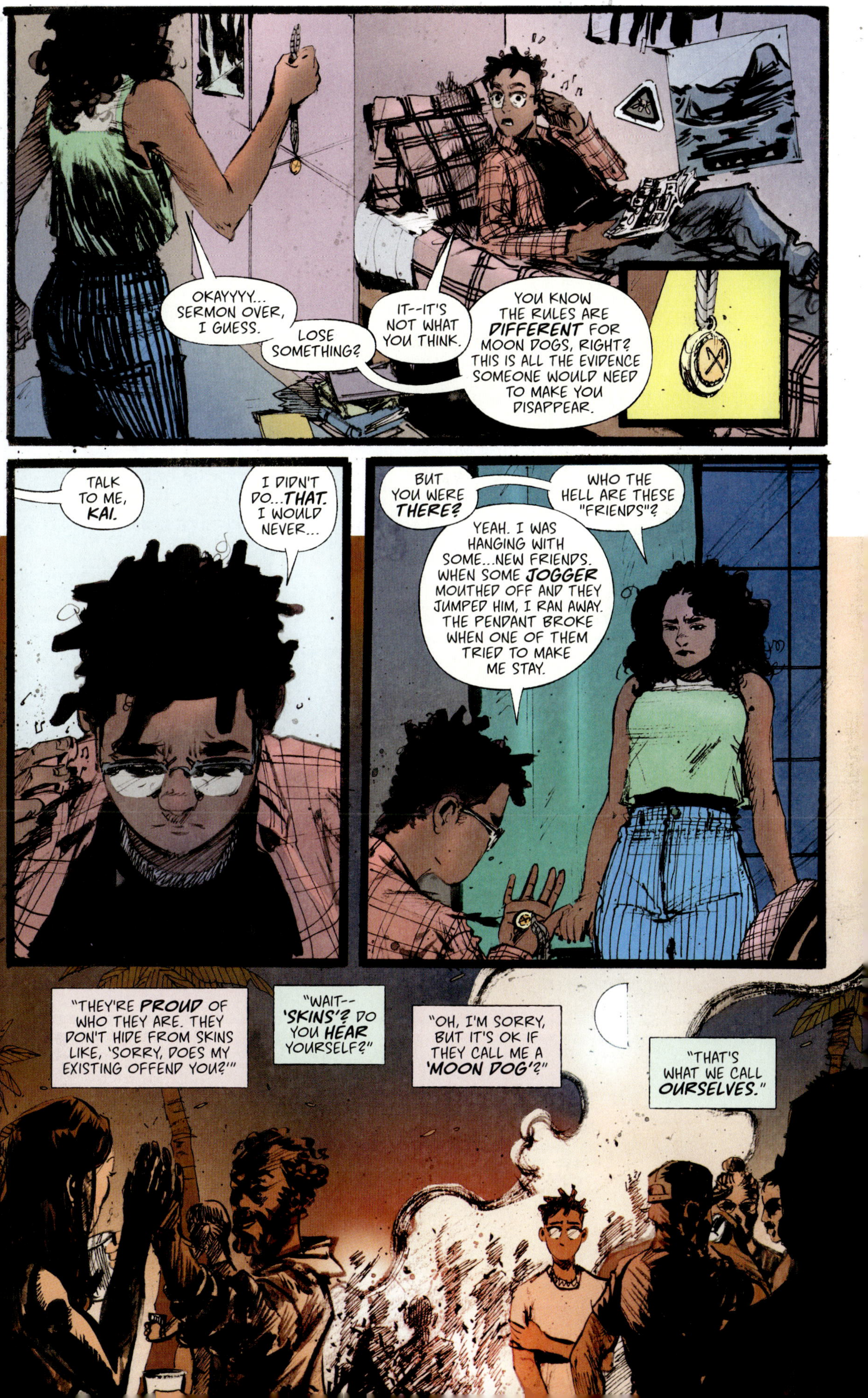
OKAYYYY... SERMON OVER, I GUESS.
LOSE SOMETHING?
IT--IT'S NOT WHAT YOU THINK.
YOU KNOW THE RULES ARE DIFFERENT FOR MOON DOGS, RIGHT? THIS IS ALL THE EVIDENCE SOMEONE WOULD NEED TO MAKE YOU DISAPPEAR.
TALK TO ME, KAI.
I DIDN'T DO...THAT. I WOULD NEVER...
BUT YOU WERE THERE?
WHO THE HELL ARE THESE "FRIENDS"?
YEAH. I WAS HANGING WITH SOME...NEW FRIENDS. WHEN SOME JOGGER MOUTHED OFF AND THEY JUMPED HIM, I RAN AWAY. THE PENDANT BROKE WHEN ONE OF THEM TRIED TO MAKE ME STAY.
"THEY'RE PROUD OF WHO THEY ARE. THEY DON'T HIDE FROM SKINS LIKE, 'SORRY, DOES MY EXISTING OFFEND YOU?'"
"WAIT-- 'SKINS'? DO YOU HEAR YOURSELF?"
"OH, I'M SORRY, BUT IT'S OK IF THEY CALL ME A 'MOON DOG'?"
"THAT'S WHAT WE CALL OURSELVES."

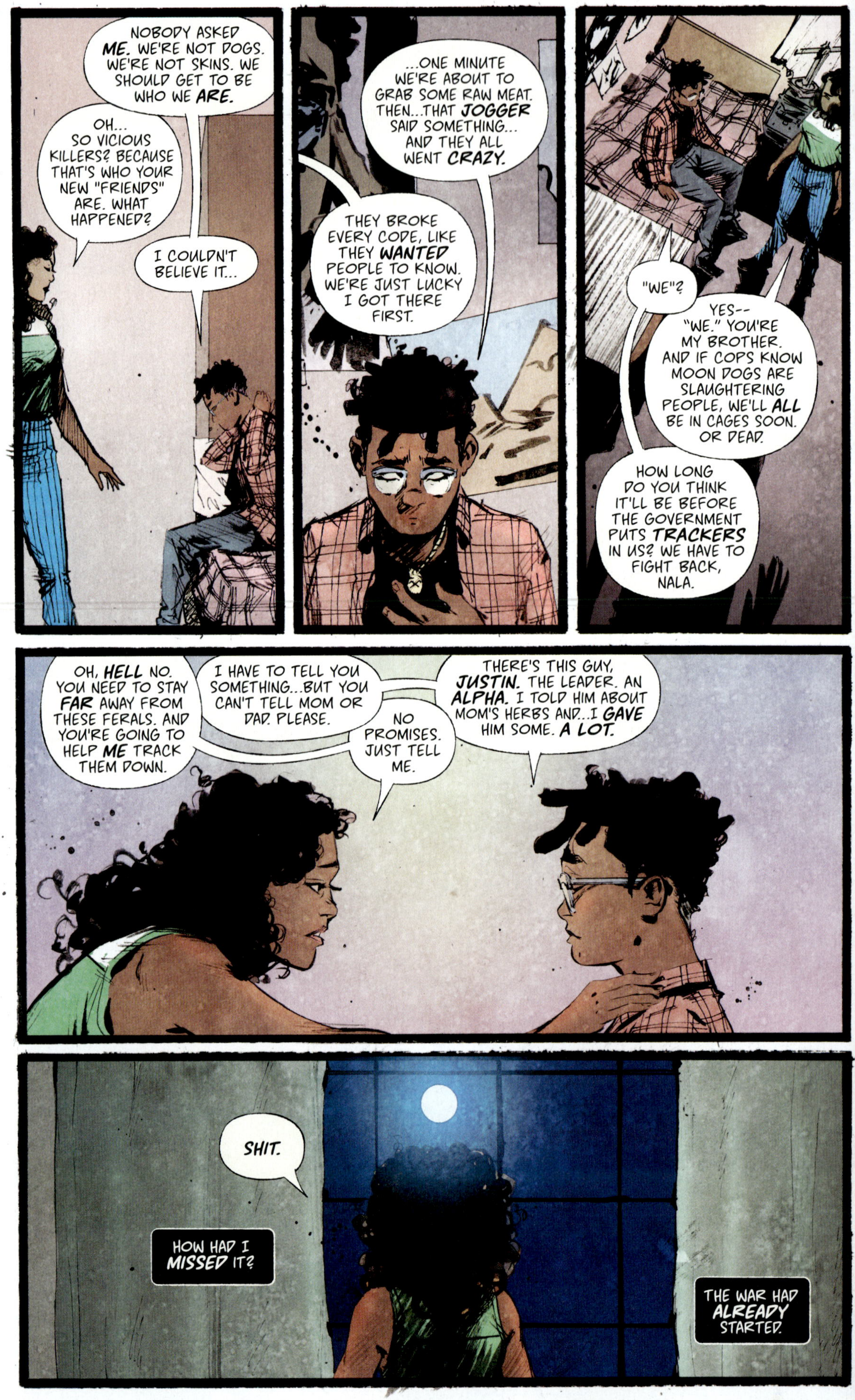
NOBODY ASKED ME. WE'RE NOT DOGS. WE'RE NOT SKINS. WE SHOULD GET TO BE WHO WE ARE.
OH... SO VICIOUS KILLERS? BECAUSE THAT'S WHO YOUR NEW "FRIENDS" ARE. WHAT HAPPENED?
I COULDN'T BELIEVE IT...
...ONE MINUTE WE'RE ABOUT TO GRAB SOME RAW MEAT. THEN...THAT JOGGER SAID SOMETHING... AND THEY ALL WENT CRAZY.
THEY BROKE EVERY CODE, LIKE THEY WANTED PEOPLE TO KNOW. WE'RE JUST LUCKY I GOT THERE FIRST.
"WE"?
YES-- "WE." YOU'RE MY BROTHER. AND IF COPS KNOW MOON DOGS ARE SLAUGHTERING PEOPLE, WE'LL ALL BE IN CAGES SOON. OR DEAD.
HOW LONG DO YOU THINK IT'LL BE BEFORE THE GOVERNMENT PUTS TRACKERS IN US? WE HAVE TO FIGHT BACK, NALA.
I HAVE TO TELL YOU SOMETHING...BUT YOU CAN'T TELL MOM OR DAD. PLEASE.
NO PROMISES. JUST TELL ME.
THERE'S THIS GUY, JUSTIN. THE LEADER. AN ALPHA. I TOLD HIM ABOUT MOM'S HERBS AND...I GAVE HIM SOME. A LOT.
OH, HELL NO. YOU NEED TO STAY FAR AWAY FROM THESE FERALS. AND YOU'RE GOING TO HELP ME TRACK THEM DOWN.
SHIT.
HOW HAD I MISSED IT?
THE WAR HAD ALREADY STARTED.

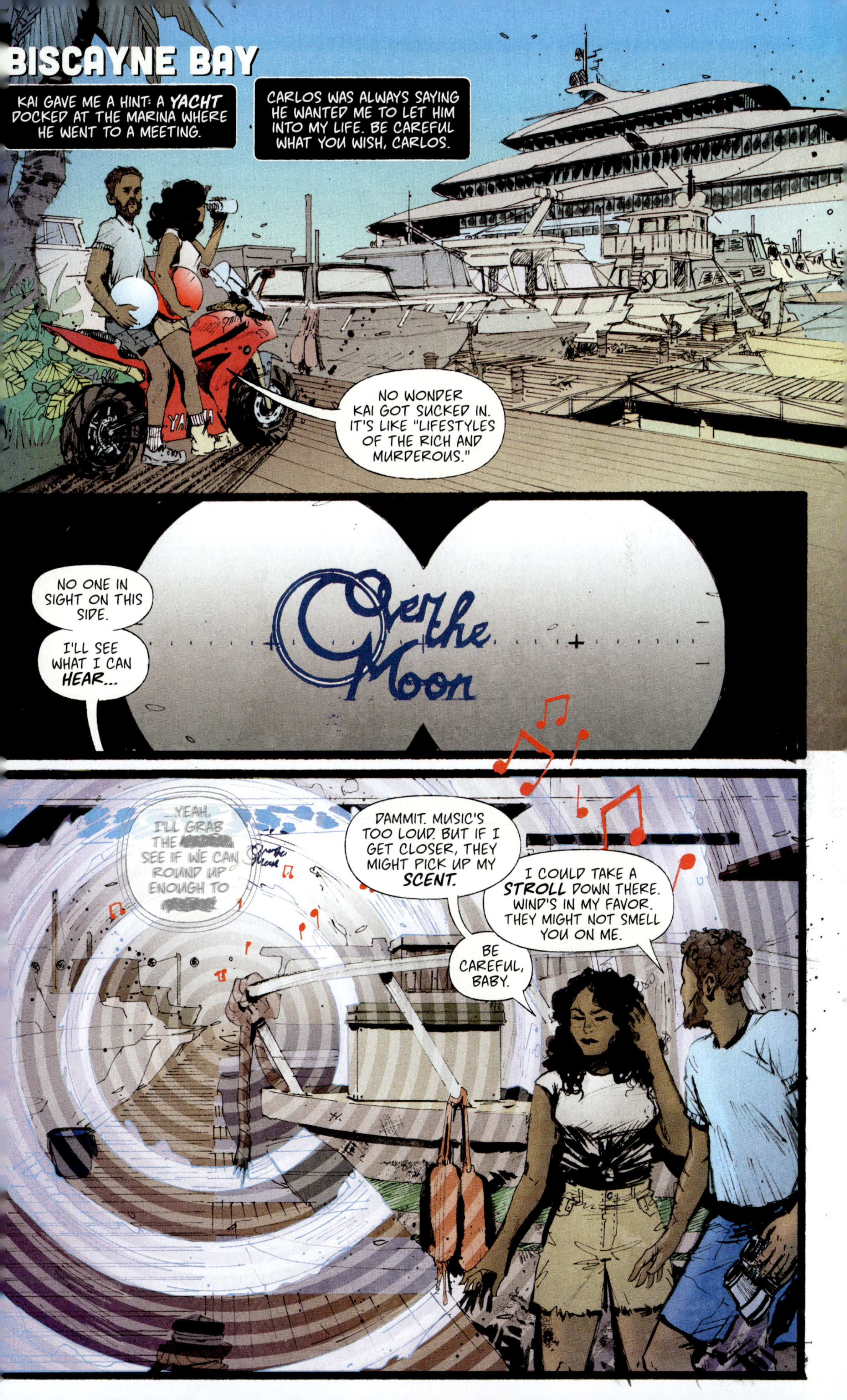
BISCAYNE BAY
KAI GAVE ME A HINT: A *YACHT* DOCKED AT THE MARINA WHERE HE WENT TO A MEETING.
CARLOS WAS ALWAYS SAYING HE WANTED ME TO LET HIM INTO MY LIFE. BE CAREFUL WHAT YOU WISH, CARLOS.
NO WONDER KAI GOT SUCKED IN. IT'S LIKE "LIFESTYLES OF THE RICH AND MURDEROUS."
NO ONE IN SIGHT ON THIS SIDE.
I'LL SEE WHAT I CAN *HEAR*...
Over the Moon
...YEAH. I'LL GRAB THE
SEE IF WE CAN ROUND UP ENOUGH TO
DAMMIT. MUSIC'S TOO LOUD. BUT IF I GET CLOSER, THEY MIGHT PICK UP MY *SCENT*.
I COULD TAKE A *STROLL* DOWN THERE. WIND'S IN MY FAVOR. THEY MIGHT NOT SMELL YOU ON ME.
BE CAREFUL, BABY.

...WHERE'S THE PARTY, MAN? I THINK I'M LOST. ALL THESE BIG-ASS YACHTS LOOK ALIKE...
...JUST DON'T KNOW IF IT'S THE RIGHT TIME.
WHAT TIME'S BETTER? THEY WON'T FUCK WITH US AFTER WHAT HAPPENS DOWN AT VIRGINIA...
DOWN AT VIRGINIA
OK, I MIGHT HAVE SOMETHING...
...BUT THIS BIG, HAIRY, SCARY DUDE IS LOOKING RIGHT AT ME...

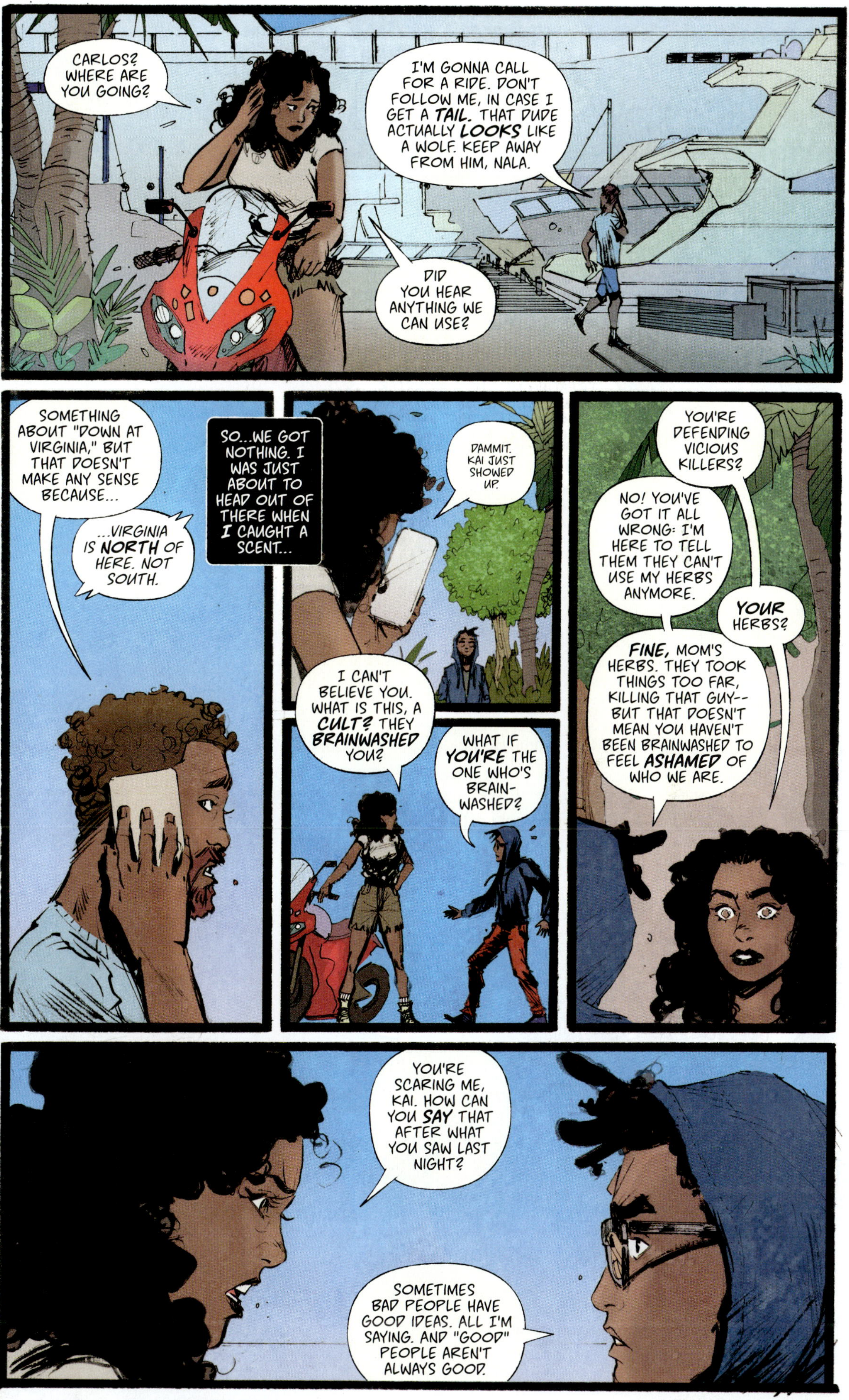

CARLOS? WHERE ARE YOU GOING?
I'M GONNA CALL FOR A RIDE. DON'T FOLLOW ME, IN CASE I GET A TAIL. THAT DUDE ACTUALLY LOOKS LIKE A WOLF. KEEP AWAY FROM HIM, NALA.
DID YOU HEAR ANYTHING WE CAN USE?
SOMETHING ABOUT "DOWN AT VIRGINIA," BUT THAT DOESN'T MAKE ANY SENSE BECAUSE...
...VIRGINIA IS NORTH OF HERE. NOT SOUTH.
SO...WE GOT NOTHING. I WAS JUST ABOUT TO HEAD OUT OF THERE WHEN I CAUGHT A SCENT...
DAMMIT. KAI JUST SHOWED UP.
I CAN'T BELIEVE YOU. WHAT IS THIS, A CULT? THEY BRAINWASHED YOU?
WHAT IF YOU'RE THE ONE WHO'S BRAIN-WASHED?
YOU'RE DEFENDING VICIOUS KILLERS?
NO! YOU'VE GOT IT ALL WRONG: I'M HERE TO TELL THEM THEY CAN'T USE MY HERBS ANYMORE.
YOUR HERBS?
FINE, MOM'S HERBS. THEY TOOK THINGS TOO FAR, KILLING THAT GUY--BUT THAT DOESN'T MEAN YOU HAVEN'T BEEN BRAINWASHED TO FEEL ASHAMED OF WHO WE ARE.
YOU'RE SCARING ME, KAI. HOW CAN YOU SAY THAT AFTER WHAT YOU SAW LAST NIGHT?
SOMETIMES BAD PEOPLE HAVE GOOD IDEAS. ALL I'M SAYING. AND "GOOD" PEOPLE AREN'T ALWAYS GOOD.

I COULDN'T INVITE CARLOS TO DINNER ON MOON NIGHTS. "FAMILY" ONLY. TRUST ME...HE WOULDN'T LIKE THE MENU.
BLESS THESE CREATURES FOR OUR SUSTENANCE. MAY WE ALWAYS EQUALLY HONOR THE SKIN WE'RE IN...AND OUR LINEAGE OF FUR AND FANG.
MAY THIS MOON NIGHT BRING US CLOSER TO OUR ANCESTRAL POWER...WHILE OUR TEA TEMPERS OUR SPIRITS WITH PEACE.
GRRRR
CHMPP
CHOMP
CHLOP
CARLOS WOULDN'T LIKE OUR TABLE MANNERS, EITHER. I WAS NERVOUS ABOUT HIM EVER SEEING ALL OF WHO WE ARE. BUT I HAD OTHER THINGS TO WORRY ABOUT...LIKE MY BROTHER.
AND WONDERING WHAT THOSE FERALS HAVE PLANNED FOR MOON NIGHT. BUT MOM AND DAD PLANNED DINNER AND A SHOW...

WHERE I GREW UP, EVERYONE LIVED IN FEAR OF THOSE WHO CROSS THEIR STAFFS. WE ALONE COULD UNLOCK THE POWER OF THE HYENA.
IN THE ARMY, I HAD A SERGEANT WHO LOVED MY SECRET THAT I WAS "A LITTLE BIT WOLF."
BUT, YOU TWO ARE THE BEST OF EACH OF US!
WE HAVE ALL THIS POWER, SO WHY CAN'T WE CLAIM OUR RIGHTFUL PLACE?
WE CAN'T THINK LIKE THAT, SON.
OUR GIFT IS NOT FOR DOMINION. IT IS OUR SACRED RESPONSIBILITY TO BE STRONG ONLY WHEN WE'RE NEEDED.
SOMEHOW, I MANAGED TO SLEEP, BUT I WOKE UP WITH A BAD FEELING...
AND WHEN I SAW KAI'S BED HADN'T BEEN SLEPT IN...

I KNEW KAI WOULDN'T LIKE WHAT I WAS ABOUT TO TELL HIM AFTER DINNER.
TEA MIGHT NOT WORK
THAT'S MY SISTER'S FRIEND!
PLEASE--LET HIM GO! THIS ISN'T WHY I GAVE YOU THE HERBS!
SHUT UP, BOY!
THIS COP WILL BE THE SACRIFICE THAT SETS US FREE! ONCE THEY FIND OUT A BUNCH OF "FERALS" TOOK ONE OF THEIR OWN, COPS WILL BE TRYING TO ROUND UP AND SHOOT EVERY MOON DOG THEY SEE!
THEN MORE OF OUR KIND WILL LISTEN TO MY MESSAGE: IT'S US VERSUS THEM! WE CAN HAVE TRUE POWER-- FIRST IN THIS CITY, THEN THE WORLD OVER. NO MORE HIDING! NO MORE SCRAPS!
THANKS TO THE HERBS THAT HELP US CONTROL OUR FORM, ANYONE WHO STANDS UP TO US WILL FACE OUR WRATH--NOT THE OTHER WAY AROUND!
NOT SO FAST!

THE HERBS DON'T BELONG TO YOU: THEY BELONG TO ME!
GRRROOOWWWLL

I KNOW THIS FEELS WRONG IN EVERY WAY. BUT WE CAN'T HAVE HIS BODY SHOW UP WITH **CLAW MARKS.**
SORRY, LUIS. YOU DESERVED BETTER.
I JUST WANTED TO FIND A WAY TO MAKE LIFE **BETTER** FOR US. I DIDN'T KNOW SHARING THE HERBS COULD GO SO WRONG... SO **FAST.**
DON'T WORRY: WE'LL FIGURE OUT HOW TO BUILD THAT FUTURE YOU WANT. **TOGETHER.**
I COULDN'T BRING MYSELF TO TELL KAI THAT HE WAS RIGHT: MOON DOGS **WOULD** NEED TO PROTECT OURSELVES.
BUT IT WOULD MEAN TRUSTING PEOPLE LIKE CARLOS TO BE ON OUR SIDE.
AND TRUSTING **FAMILY** TO HAVE EACH OTHER'S BACKS, NO MATTER WHAT.
WHATEVER LAY AHEAD, WE WERE **ALL** RIDING INTO OUR FUTURE TOGETHER.
END

WOULD PEOPLE STILL LOVE OF US IF THEY KNEW EVERYTHING ABOUT US—

—or would we be outcasts?

What roles are we forced to play to "fit in" with society? And how does that mute our true power?

In earlier generations of African-Americans, those with fair skin could "pass" for white. Boots Riley's brilliant film *Sorry to Bother You* showcases the phenomenon of "code switching" and "white voice"—the survival tactic of adapting different speech patterns depending on the setting. Because of homophobia, in the queer community many people still feel compelled to hide their sexuality from friends, family members, and co-workers.

Too many of us relate to not feeling truly seen—and yet being afraid to reveal who we really are in all our complexities because others might not understand us.

This was the seed of inspiration that led to Nala's character in MOON DOGS—a young woman from a mixed family, but one like we haven't seen: her father is a werewolf from the United States and her mother is a were-hyena from Somalia.

And of course it's Miami. Miami is in my blood.

It's where I grew up. It's where I first had my first job as a reporter for *The Miami Herald*. And it's the setting for one of my most popular novels: *My Soul to Keep*, about Ethiopian immortals, which is like a vampire myth through a Looking Glass.

This time, I want to revisit our understanding of Werewolves.

What is it like to feel outcast, especially for a Black werewolf who is a minority within a minority? How can creatures with an unfair advantage over others convince themselves to use restraint? What does "identity" mean to a werewolf?

In future comics, Lycanthropes could be thrust into the public eye, subject to the rules, tracking and scrutiny Kai was afraid of. Nala—or even Kai—could rise to a leadership position during an inevitable war between humans and Lycanthropes. And her family's herbal blend might fall into the wrong hands outside of Nala's family—and this time, Nala, Carlos, and her family may be unable to stop a plan by Ferals to rule humans. Or will Nala herself be corrupted by the power of the herbs to control her transformations?

In MOON DOGS, Lycanthropes live in secrecy, but have an International Collective.

But the secret is getting out. And Nala's family herbs have the potential to change the way the world sees Lycanthropes forever—either for good or ill.

My husband, Steven Barnes, and I co-authored a graphic novel called *The Keeper* adapting one of our screenplays, but I am very new to comics. The process of bringing a story to life through images and colors, not just words, is still very novel and, frankly, mind-blowing to me.

I must shout out my collaborators on MOON DOGS: My artist collaborator, Kelsey Ramsay, who made me homesick with her images of Miami and made the story so visceral and rich. And also colorist José Villarrubia, who took those images and infused them with glorious color. And letterer Jeff Powell, who also did a fantastic job telling the story down to the letter.

A special note of thanks to editors Pornsak Pichethote and Will Dennis for giving me the opportunity to be a part of THE HORIZON EXPERIMENT.

It's a privilege to learn this new medium with such exciting professionals. (And if you'll excuse me...I think tonight might be a Moon Night.)

Tananarive Due

Tananarive Due

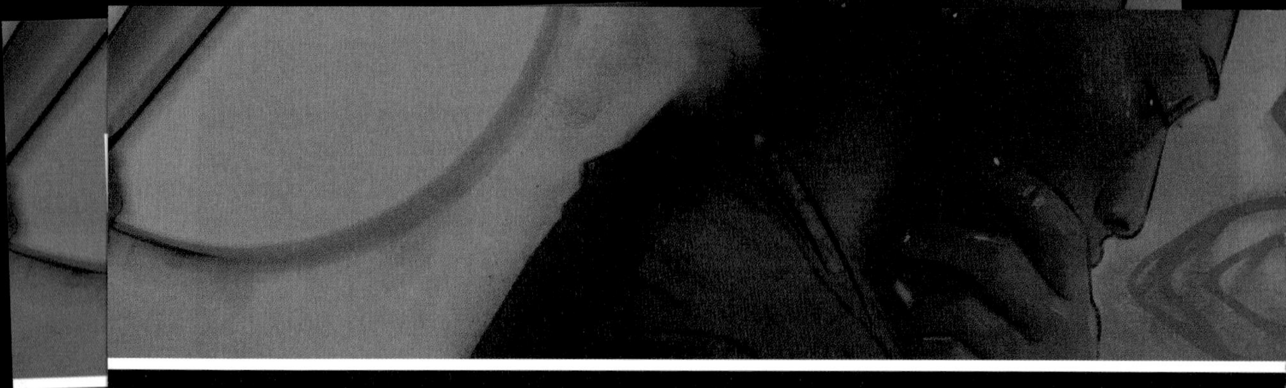

"MOTHERFU*KIN MONSTERS is motherfu*kin' great! A fun balance of horror and humor—I can't wait to see what happens next for JJ and his friends."

—DAVID F. WALKER
(BITTER ROOT, *Big Jim and the White Boy*)

"A lot of motherf*kin' fun! A cool mix of giggles and gore, with sharp, memorable characters and some truly great cartooning. The Satanically-possessed comic book love-child of Jordan Peele and Sam Raimi."

—JOHN LAYMAN
(CHEW, THE SCORCHED)

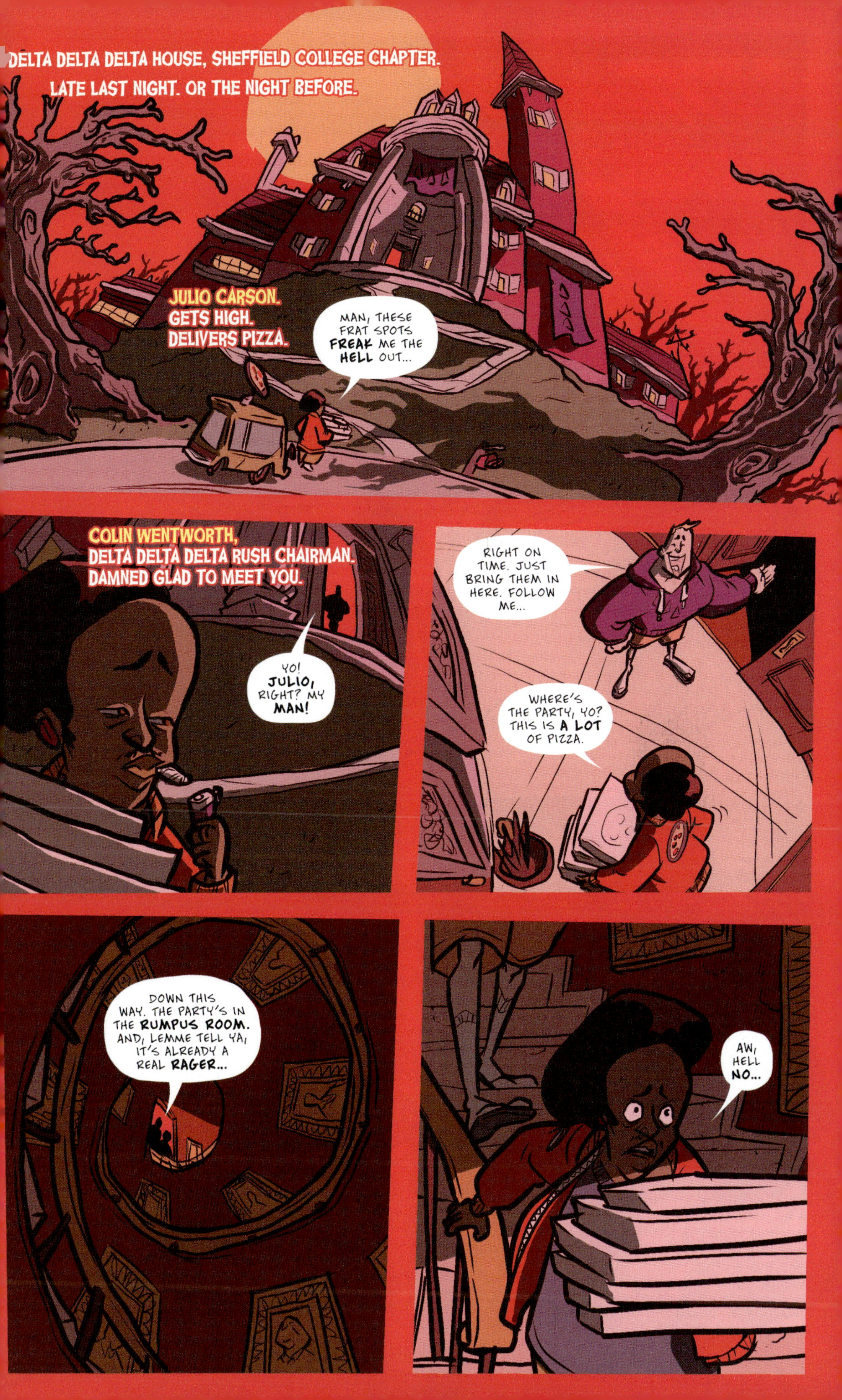
DELTA DELTA DELTA HOUSE, SHEFFIELD COLLEGE CHAPTER.
LATE LAST NIGHT. OR THE NIGHT BEFORE.
JULIO CARSON. GETS HIGH. DELIVERS PIZZA.
MAN, THESE FRAT SPOTS FREAK ME THE HELL OUT...
COLIN WENTWORTH, DELTA DELTA DELTA RUSH CHAIRMAN. DAMNED GLAD TO MEET YOU.
YO! JULIO, RIGHT? MY MAN!
RIGHT ON TIME. JUST BRING THEM IN HERE. FOLLOW ME...
WHERE'S THE PARTY, YO? THIS IS A LOT OF PIZZA.
DOWN THIS WAY. THE PARTY'S IN THE RUMPUS ROOM. AND, LEMME TELL YA, IT'S ALREADY A REAL RAGER...
AW, HELL NO...

THE "RUMPUS" ROOM.
THE DELTA DELTA DELTA BROTHERS.
...FOR REAL, DUDE?
THE GRIMOIRE.
DON'T YOU KNOW IN THE HORROR MOVIE...
...THE BLACK GUY ALWAYS GETS IT FIRST.
SLICE

SPLASH
DON'T WORRY. YOU'LL HAVE MORE COMPANY **SOON.**
EAT UP, MY DUDES. 'CAUSE REMEMBER... THE **REAL** PARTY IS COMING.
WUMP
THUMP
IT'S NOT A **PARTY,** COLIN.
IT'S A **RECKONING.** THE DARK SPIRITS ARE **HUNGRY,** BUT OUR FIRST OFFERING HAS BEEN ACCEPTED. THE DOOR IS BEGINNING TO OPEN.
AND **WHO** WILL BE ABLE TO STAND AGAINST **US?**

TODAY.
SHEFFIELD COLLEGE. UPSTATE NEW YORK. 115 MILES FROM BROOKLYN.
JJ HENRY. OUR HERO. SORTA.
'SUP, FAM!

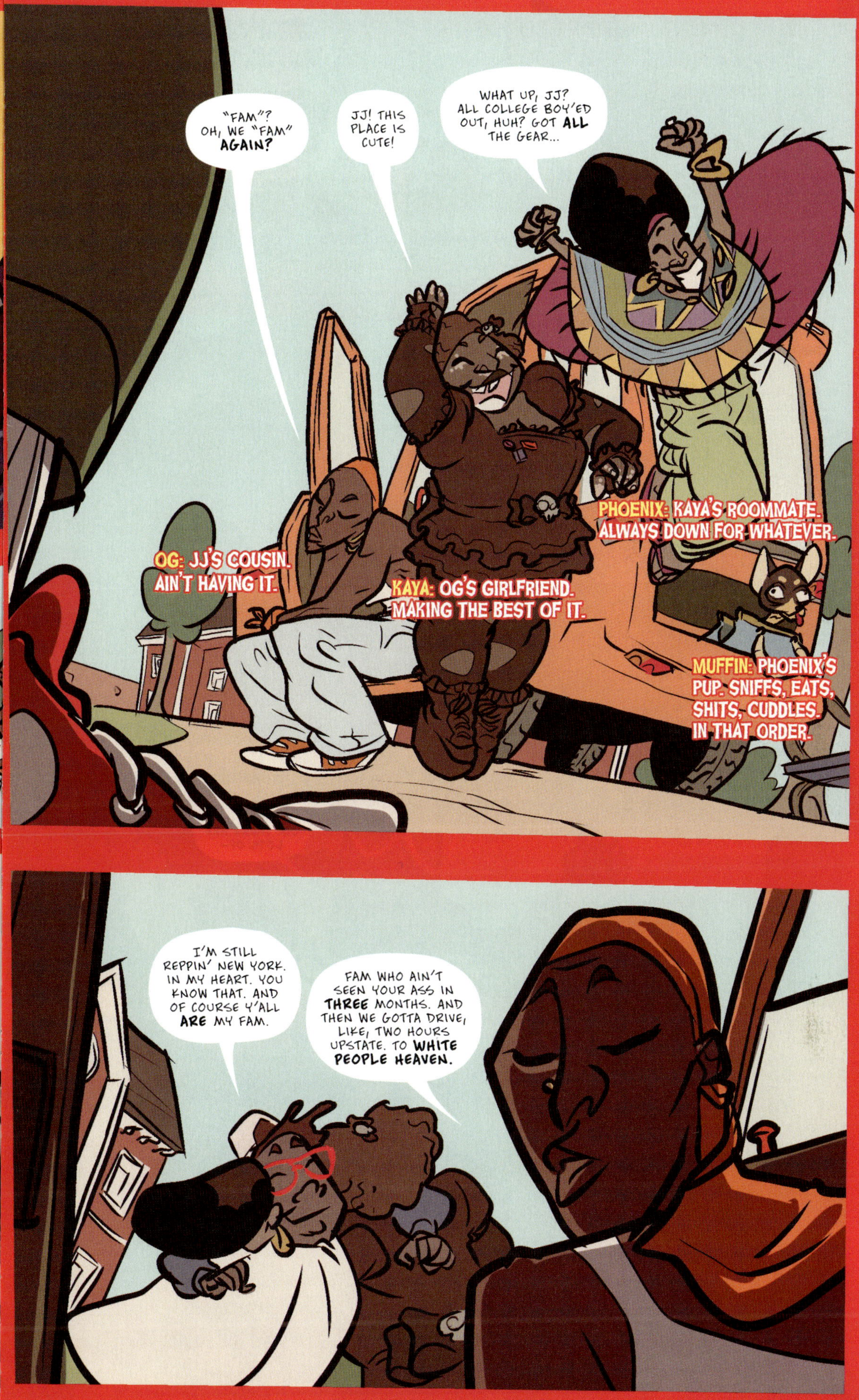
"FAM"? OH, WE "FAM" **AGAIN?**
JJ! THIS PLACE IS CUTE!
WHAT UP, JJ? ALL COLLEGE BOY'ED OUT, HUH? GOT **ALL** THE GEAR...
PHOENIX: KAYA'S ROOMMATE. ALWAYS DOWN FOR WHATEVER.
OG: JJ'S COUSIN. AIN'T HAVING IT.
KAYA: OG'S GIRLFRIEND. MAKING THE BEST OF IT.
MUFFIN: PHOENIX'S PUP. SNIFFS, EATS, SHITS, CUDDLES. IN THAT ORDER.
I'M STILL REPPIN' NEW YORK. IN MY HEART. YOU KNOW THAT. AND OF COURSE Y'ALL **ARE** MY FAM.
FAM WHO AIN'T SEEN YOUR ASS IN **THREE** MONTHS. AND THEN WE GOTTA DRIVE, LIKE, TWO HOURS UPSTATE. TO **WHITE PEOPLE HEAVEN.**

THEY HAD A LONG DRIVE. THEY'RE ALL **TIRED.** JUST GONNA GET THEM TO MY DORM TO HANG OUT...
BUT YOU'RE STILL COMING BY THE MIXER TONIGHT? WE'RE ALL LOOKING FORWARD TO GETTING TO KNOW YOU BETTER.
DELTA HOUSE
TONIGHT!
ALL ARE
WELCOME!
IS THAT **TONIGHT?** HUH. I TOTALLY FORGOT...
YOU GOTTA BE THERE! WHO ELSE IS GONNA TEACH US TO PLAY DUNGEONS & DRAGONS?
JJ'S A **KAPPA** LEGACY. GOING BACK **THREE** GENERATIONS. HE DOESN'T NEED SOME DELTA **BULLSHIT.**
...KAPPA? I DON'T THINK I KNOW **THAT ONE...**
OKAY, COOL, YEAH, I'LL SEE YOU TONIGHT, COLIN! CAN'T WAIT!
YEAH, OKAY...
NICE TO MEET YOU! SAY GOODBYE, MUFFIN!

WHAT COULD SOME DUSTY, CRUSTY, WHITE-ASS FRAT HAVE FOR YOU? IT'S BAD ENOUGH YOU'RE HERE AT-
YOU ALREADY CALLED IT "WHITE PEOPLE HEAVEN," SO YOU'LL NEED A NEW LINE. AND DELTA IS THE BEST FRAT ON CAMPUS. EVERYONE WANTS TO GET INTO IT. AND THEY'RE NOT BAD GUYS.
TIME OUT. YOU TWO AREN'T GONNA FIGHT LIKE THIS THE WHOLE TIME WE'RE HERE, ARE YOU? 'CAUSE THAT AIN'T FUN FOR ANYONE.
I DON'T KNOW WHY Y'ALL CAME UP HERE IF YOU'RE JUST GONNA BE MEAN TO ME THE WHOLE TIME.
NEGRO, WE CAME UP HERE BECAUSE WE'RE YOUR FAMILY AND FRIENDS AND YOU JUST LEFT US ALL HIGH AND DRY.
WHAT OG IS TRYING TO SAY IS THAT SHE CARES ABOUT YOU AND SHE MISSED YOU AND SHE'S WORRIED THAT THIS PLACE ISN'T GOOD FOR YOU.
WE ALL MISSED YOU.

DON'T LET OG GET TO YOU, MAN. SHE'S MOSTLY JUST TALKING.
SHE'S ALWAYS RIDING ME. ALWAYS POKING AT ME. LIKE I'M NEVER GOOD ENOUGH.
YOU KNOW I NEVER FIT IN, BACK IN BUSHWICK. I WAS A HERB, A NERD, A WEIRDO. A COMIC BOOK GEEK. BUT UP HERE, PEOPLE LIKE THAT I'M SMART. THEY GET IT. MOSTLY.
I ALWAYS LIKED THAT YOU'RE SMART.
YEAH, BUT YOU'RE A WEIRDO. LIKE ME. YOU JUST DO, LIKE, ASTROLOGY INSTEAD OF SUPERHEROES.
MR. HENRY. IS THIS YOUR... MESS?
OH. SORRY, PROFESSOR RANDOLPH. MY FRIEND WAS JUST GONNA GRAB THAT.
I SHOULD HOPE SO.
AH, PLANNING TO ATTEND ONE OF THE DELTA'S BACCHANALS TONIGHT?
MIXER at DELTA HOUSE

I WAS THINKING ABOUT IT. THEY'RE TRYING TO RECRUIT ME **HARD.**
YOU SHOULD BE **CAREFUL** ABOUT WHO YOU ASSOCIATE WITH, MR. HENRY. YOU HAVE A BRIGHT **FUTURE.** I'D HATE FOR YOU TO THROW IT ALL AWAY BY SPENDING YOUR TIME WITH THE WRONG **ELEMENTS.**
I'M JUST TRYING TO FIT IN. I REALLY WANT TO DO WELL HERE.
YOUR TIME WILL COME, MR. HENRY. I KNOW IT.
WHO **WAS** THAT DUDE?
HISTORY PROFESSOR.
LOOKS LIKE A FREAKING **CREEP.**
GOTTA BE SCORPIO WITH A GEMINI MOON. **BAD** NEWS ALL OVER.

MAYBE Y'ALL SHOULD JUST **GO.** YOU **HATE** THIS PLACE, YOU **HATE** ALL THE PEOPLE. YOU **HATE** **ME.** OBVIOUSLY.
WE **DON'T.** YOU **KNOW** WE DON'T.
WE **CARE** ABOUT YOU. WE'RE JUST **WATCHING** OUT FOR YOU.
I CAN WATCH OUT FOR **MYSELF.**
WE'RE **FAMILY.** SO YOU'RE STUCK WITH US. NO MATTER WHAT.
SIGH
MAYBE THIS DELTA PARTY WILL BE...**OKAY.**
YES!
I THINK Y'ALL WILL HAVE A GOOD TIME!

TONIGHT.
YOU CALL THIS FUN?
IT'S JUST GETTING STARTED.
THE DRINKS ARE DECENT.
I THOUGHT YOU SAID THERE WEREN'T ANY BLACK FOLK HERE.
HUH. YEAH, I GUESS. LOT OF INTERNATIONAL STUDENTS AND STUFF. KINDA MAKES SENSE, THOUGH...
"MAKES SENSE"?
WHAT MAKES SENSE?
WHAT DIDN'T YOU TELL US?

WELL. DELTA HAD THIS WHOLE, LIKE, **ISSUE** WITH TURNING AWAY SOME, UH, MINORITY APPLICANTS. AND, LIKE, THE SCHOOL MADE THEM DO, LIKE, **REPARATIONS.** SO...THAT'S WHAT THIS IS ABOUT.
YOU BROUGHT US TO SOME KIND OF **"WE AREN'T THE KLAN"** RALLY?
NOT **COOL,** JJ.
GRRRRR!
REPARATIONS ISN'T THE RIGHT WORD HERE.
I JUST WANTED YOU TO SEE THAT THEY AREN'T SO **BAD!** THEY'RE **TRYING!**
JJ, YOU **WRONG.** AND YOU KNOW YOU **WRONG.** I LOVE YOU, BUT THIS WHOLE THING IS GODDAMN **WRONG.** WE **OUT.**
YOU KNOW **YOU'RE** BETTER THAN THIS.
YOU CAN'T LEAVE. THE **FESTIVITIES** ARE JUST ABOUT TO START...

BROTHERS, LET'S PARTY.
AHHHH!
THEY'RE FUCKING KILLING EVERYONE.
ARGHHHH!
NOOOOO!
WHAT THE FUCK?
I TOLD YOU, JJ. I TOLD YOU AND TOLD YOU. YOU CAN'T TRUST THESE PEOPLE!
FACTS: NEVER TRUST WHITE BOYS.
TRUE THAT.
WHITE PEOPLE ALWAYS BRING SOME BULLSHIT. I'M NEVER LEAVING BROOKLYN AGAIN.
I REALLY THOUGHT THEY WERE OKAY!

ACCEPT OUR OFFERINGS, DARK LORDS, AND GRANT US POWER...
AW...
...SHIT...
HUUUUMMMMMMMM
GROWWWWLLLL
GROWWL
OH, FUCK...
...THIS!

CANNOT TRUST THESE...
...MOTHER-FUCKING...
...WHITE BOYS!

WE OUTTA HERE. NOW.
YOU THINK YOU'RE SO FUCKING SMART.
KRACK
I KNOW I'M FUCKING SMART!
JJ! THE BOOK! GET TO THE BOOK!
ON IT!

YES, MR. HENRY. YOU **ARE** ON IT.
PEOPLE LIKE THAT, THEY'LL JUST HOLD YOU BACK. IT'S TIME TO EMBRACE YOUR **DESTINY**.
PROFESSOR **RANDOLPH?**
YOU CAME HERE TO BETTER YOURSELF. THIS WILL MAKE YOU **BETTER. STRONGER.** TO GAIN **POWER.** AND EMBRACE YOUR **DESTINY.** THIS CAN DO ALL OF THAT. AND **MORE...**
JUST REACH OUT AND TAKE MY **HAND.** AND JOIN YOUR NEW **FAMILY...**
DON'T, JJ!

YOUR CLASS SUCKS, DUDE.
GET YOUR HANDS OFF OF IT!
TEAARRRRR!
AAAAAHHHHH!
BOOM!

TAKE THIS POWER, MY CHILDREN, AND USE IT TO CLEANSE THIS WORLD OF ALL OF THE FILTH... EVERYWHERE!
OH. SHIT.
MOREHOUSE
AHHHHHH!
GRRRRR
Howard University
SPELLMAN

WE GOTTA GO. COME ON, COME ON, COME ON...
I SAW... I SAW WHAT THEY WANT TO DO. WHAT THEY'RE GONNA DO...
PHOENIX, COME ON!
MUFFIN! WHERE'S MUFFIN?
HOLY SHIT... THIS IS ALL SO FUCKED...THERE ARE THREE OTHER BOOKS. IF THEY GET ALL OF THEM...
MOVE YOUR ASS!
WE CAN'T LET THEM WIN!
I'M SORRY. I WAS ACTING LIKE A JACKASS BEFORE.
YOU WERE JUST DOING WHAT YOU THOUGHT WAS RIGHT. WHAT YOU THOUGHT YOU HAD TO DO.
WELL, NOW I KNOW BETTER.
GLAD Y'ALL HAVE MADE UP... BUT WE HAVE GOT TO GO!

I THOUGHT HAVING ONE OF **THEM** ON OUR SIDE, AS **OUR** PUPPET, WOULD BE A GREAT ADVANTAGE. BUT WE'RE NOT **FINISHED** WITH HIM AND HIS FRIENDS JUST YET...
I KNEW HE WOULD **SCREW** IT ALL UP. I **KNEW** IT.
COLIN...?
AND HE'S **GONNA** PAY FOR IT...IN **BLOOD**...
MUFFIN! THERE YOU ARE! COME ON, BABY!
CRRRRRRRRRRR
OH, **NO.** OH, **NO.**
URRRP
PHOENIX, MOVE YOUR ASS! NOW!
WE HAVE TO GO AND SAVE THE **WORLD!**
YEAH, YEAH, SURE, WHATEVER! LET'S GET OUT OF HERE BEFORE...

FREEZE!
THIS...
...IS...
...SOME...
BULLSHIT.
TO BE CONTINUED...

I WAS A SCAREDY CAT KID

Frightened of my own shadow, frightened of monsters in my closet, frightened of pretty much everything. If I was watching anything, a movie, a TV show, even a commercial, the scary music would start and I'd be hiding behind my hands.

But then I went to see *Evil Dead II* in an old, falling-down movie palace in Ridgewood, Queens. And all that changed. I can't remember exactly why I wanted to see that particular movie, maybe it was something about the poster, the human eyes looking out from a skull. That intrigued me. So me and a buddy went to a matinee, practically in the theatre by ourselves.

And I was hooked. I laughed. I screamed. I was scared af. But I watched the whole thing. Every single second. After that, I was a hardcore *Fangoria* kid. All horror movies, all the time, the bloodier the better. My new gods were Clive Barker, John Carpenter, Wes Craven. It's hard to find a better time for a young horror fan than the late 1980s.

But as a BLACK horror fan, well, the pickings were a lot slimmer. You had to be content with a jive-talking car thief or a bespectacled nerd who never made it past the first reel. Horror was a pretty white space.

Jump ahead to the 21st century and…horror is still a pretty white space. Even though, for most Black folks, life in America is a kind of constant horror show. So when my good friend Pornsak approached me about contributing to this very cool project and taking on a genre that typically isn't too friendly to people of color, I knew I wanted to get freaky and bring the horror.

And he let me do my thing. And then the absolutely brilliant Michael Lee Harris brought it with stunning character design and art.

MOTHERFU*KIN' MONSTERS is *Evil Dead* but for blerds. As a lifelong horror fan, I wanted to take the Black characters from sidekicks and quick deaths and put them in the center of the story. This is my love letter to Sam Raimi and Edgar Wright, set to a Wu-Tang soundtrack.

I imagine this book as a road trip through the darkest parts of the American id, uncovering all kinds of monsters, many of them hiding in plain sight. JJ, his cousin OG, her girlfriend Kaya and their dippy friend Phoenix travel across the country, trying to destroy evil grimoires that a conspiracy of white supremacists are using to wipe Black folk from the face of the earth. They'll have zombie frat boys, demented librarians and demonic cops on their trail.

And, along the way, JJ will have to decide what kind of future he wants for himself. Is there a way for him to feel at home as a Black man in a country that's literally trying to eat him alive? I certainly hope so…but, if I'm honest, I'm scared to find out that answer…

J. Holtham

FINDERS/ KEEPERS

I've been dying to work with **Vita Ayala**. A queer Afro-Puerto Rican writer out of New York City, Vita is constantly and consistently in demand, having worked on some of the most iconic franchises currently published, from the *X-Men* to *Wonder Woman* to *James Bond* to *Batman* to *Static Shock* to *Star Wars*. FINDERS/KEEPERS marks their long-awaited return to original, creator-owned work.

Speaking of dying to work with, **Skylar Patridge** has in a very short time made herself a fan-favorite comic artist, illustrator, designer, and occasional writer. She's balanced creator-owned and superhero work, from *Relics of Youth* and *Resonant* (both for Vault Comics) while also drawing some of pop culture's most beloved characters, including Batman, Wonder Woman, Supergirl, and Buffy the Vampire Slayer.

She's reunited here with colorist **Jason Wordie**, who's credited on hundreds of comics in a career that's spanned over a decade working with such celebrated artists as Wes Craig and Geoff Shaw or on such beloved properties as *Planet of the Apes* or *Harley Quinn*.

Lettering and logo design on FINDERS/KEEPERS by **Becca Carey**, who I, of course, talked about earlier.

FINDERS //
KEEPERS
image
1
JAN
$3.99
US
AYALA
PATRIDGE
WORDIE
CAREY
THE
HORIZON
EXPERIMENT

"A wild, wicked mirror-image Indiana Jones for the 21st century.
I want EVERY museum raided!"

—PATTON OSWALT
(actor/comedian/writer, *Minor Threats*, *King of Queens*)

"I can't think of many things more important—in these cynical times—than stories about exploration and adventure. After all, that's the beating heart of a call to action. FINDERS / KEEPERS is one of those stories. That it also does the MOST important thing, asking the question, 'Why?' while doing so makes it even more enjoyable."

—JONATHAN HICKMAN
(*Ultimate Spider-Man*, *X-Men*)

"It's no surprise that Vita Ayala looked at the action-adventure genre, flipped it on its head and wrote a brilliant new take on it. The entire FINDERS//KEEPERS team delivered a smash Image Comics debut -- I'll be searching for more fantastic adventures from Ines."

—GERRY DUGGAN
(*X-Men*, *Deadpool*, FALLING IN LOVE ON THE PATH TO HELL)

"FINDERS/KEEPERS is both intimate and epic, a quest to reclaim stolen culture that crackles with purpose, realism, and wonder. This inspired story by Vita Ayala and breathtaking art by Skylar Partridge pull you in and take you along for the wild ride!"

—TANANARIVE DUE
(*The Reformatory*, *The Living Blood*)

"FINDERS/KEEPERS is a terrific twist on the imperialist tomb-raider trope with complex characters who kept me riveted. Highly recommended."

—MARK WAID
(*Justice League Unlimited*, *Absolute Power*)

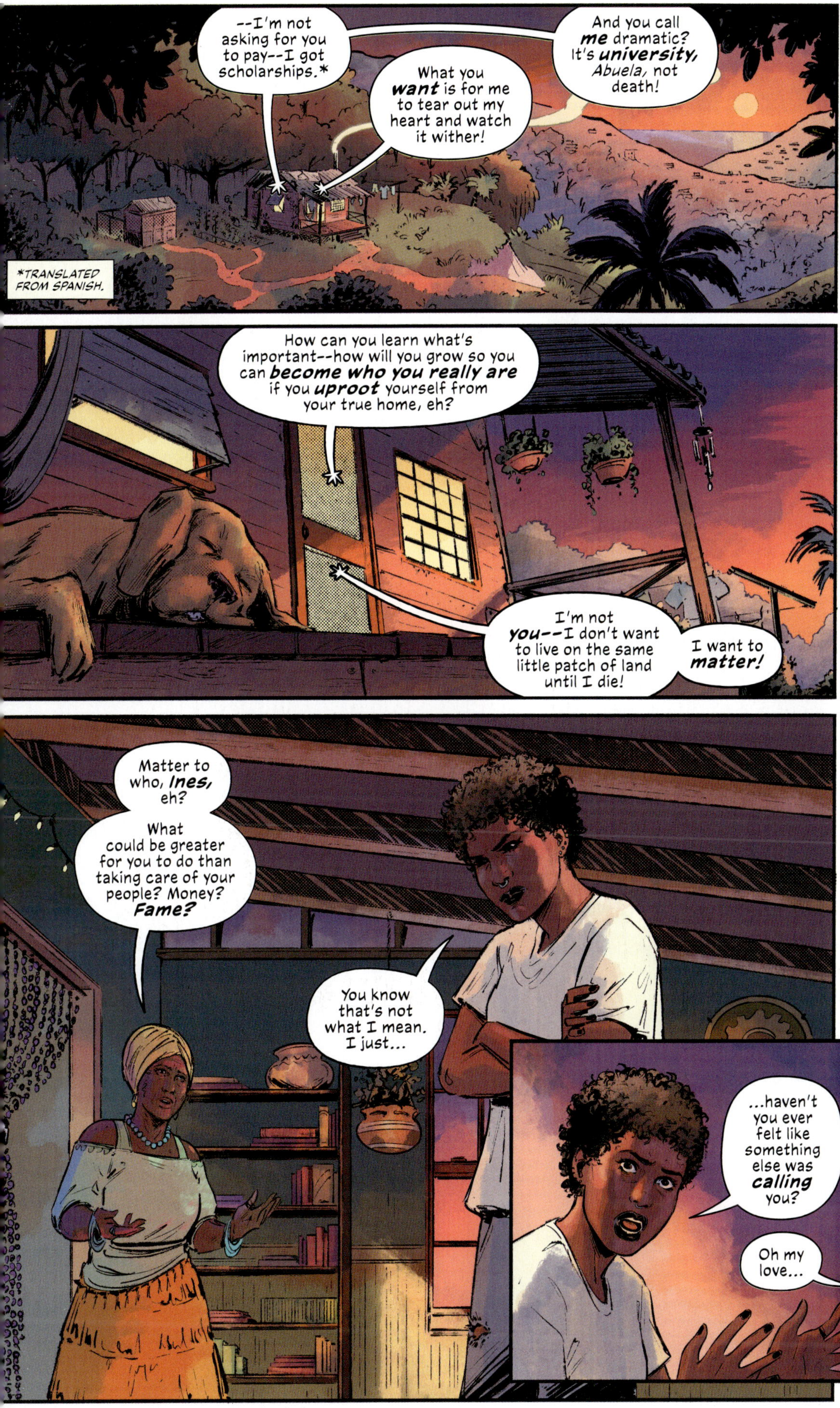
--I'm not asking for you to pay--I got scholarships.*
And you call **me** dramatic? It's **university,** *Abuela,* not death!
What you **want** is for me to tear out my heart and watch it wither!
*TRANSLATED FROM SPANISH.
How can you learn what's important--how will you grow so you can **become who you really are** if you **uproot** yourself from your true home, eh?
I'm not **you--**I don't want to live on the same little patch of land until I die!
I want to **matter!**
Matter to who, ***Ines,*** eh?
What could be greater for you to do than taking care of your people? Money? **Fame?**
You know that's not what I mean. I just...
...haven't you ever felt like something else was **calling** you?
Oh my love...

I know you feel as if the answers your heart seeks are ***out there,*** but you will be forced to squeeze yourself into boxes that will choke you until you are ***gone.***
There is no more terrible thing for one as bold of heart and beautiful of spirit as you.
You will not survive it.
Thanks for the vote of confidence!
Lucky for me, my grades at that "backwards townie school" were good enough for ***someone.***
Brown University, if that matters.
Whatever, I wasn't asking permission, I just thought maybe by some miracle you'd be proud of me.
Ines?
I'm going, ***Ana.***
I'll let you know where I land, if you even care.

WHAT TO INCLUDE IN COVER LETTER FOR MUSEUM INTERNSHIP

INTRO

- TALK ABOUT BACKGROUND, WHY ARCHEOLOGY WAS IMPORTANT TO ME, MY EARLY EXPERIENCES ON THE ISLAND THAT LED TO MY PASSION ~~(INCLUDING ABUELA'S STORIES)~~ exploiting Abuela to score points here is over the line, think of something else personal

- TALK ABOUT HOW IMPORTANT ARTIFACTS ARE FOR RECOVERING INDIGENOUS HISTORY, AND THE ROLE OF MUSEUMS IN THAT WORK

EDUCATION

- TALK ABOUT BROWN - ABOUT THE DOUBLE MAJOR IN ARCHEO AND MUSEUM STUDIES, EXTRA CURRICULAR STUDY PROJECTS, INTERNSHIPS DURING BREAKS

- TALK ABOUT BEING ALLOWED INTO A GRAD SCHOOL-LEVEL DIG INTERNSHIP AS AN UNDERGRAD AND WHAT EXPERIENCE YOU GAINED THERE

- TALK ABOUT GRAD SCHOOL AND HOW YOU WERE PUT IN CHARGE OF WRITING GRANT PROPOSALS FOR HALF THE DEPARTMENT

  this feels like too much for a section I should just be name dropping in?

- TALK ABOUT THE GONZÁLEZ FOUNDATION, HOW YOU RECEIVED MULTIPLE GRANTS, AS BOTH AN UNDERGRAD AND GRAD, HOW YOU WERE PART OF THEIR PLACEMENT PROGRAM FOR YOUR THESIS WORK

  should this be its own section???????

WORK EXPERIENCE

- BASICALLY AN "AS PER THE ATTACHED RESUME" SECTION

~~OTHER~~ ditch this section, keep it clean and more professional

- ~~TALK ABOUT PLAYING SWIMMING AND PLAYING SOCCER, AS A WAY TO SUBTLY INDICATE THAT YOU ARE USED TO LONG HOURS AND HARD WORK/TAKING ON A LOT FOR A TEAM~~

- ~~TALK ABOUT HOBBIES LIKE~~

This isn't an academic program, this is the American Art Museum to work at. This is what I've been working towards. This is EVERYTHING.

Don't let them see how much I need to get this position - don't let them see how much I gave up to get here, they will read that as weakness and desperation. Turn all that into a strength, make them think they would be losing if they let me go.

--PROTESTS HEAT UP AS WE DRAW CLOSER TO THIS YEAR'S FETE.
THE SPARK FOR THIS OUTRAGE WAS STRUCK WHEN THE THEME FOR THE BALL WAS FIRST ANNOUNCED, AND THE MUSEUM REVEALED THE CENTERPIECE WOULD BE A LONG-LOST ARTIFACT--
NEWS
LIVE
live protests at American art museum
must be a hundred protesters, most claiming
with the group, Mi Gente (a coalition of
minican, and Cuban activists operat-
clog the front stairs of the
the upcoming "Savages &
Primitive Art" show...
--KNOWN AS EL CORAZON. THE HALF OBSIDIAN-HALF WOOD OBJECT IS OF TAINO ORIGIN, RELATING BACK TO ONE OF THE CREATION MYTHS OF THE ISLAND--
--LOST AFTER THE REVOLT OF 1511--
--PROTECTORS OF BORIKEN, THE TAINO WORD FOR PUERTO RICO--
--SINK INTO THE SEA--
?
...IT CAN'T BE...
YOU STILL HERE, IDA? GUESS THAT INTAKE IS MORE INVOLVED THAN I THOUGHT!
SIGH
IT'S INES...

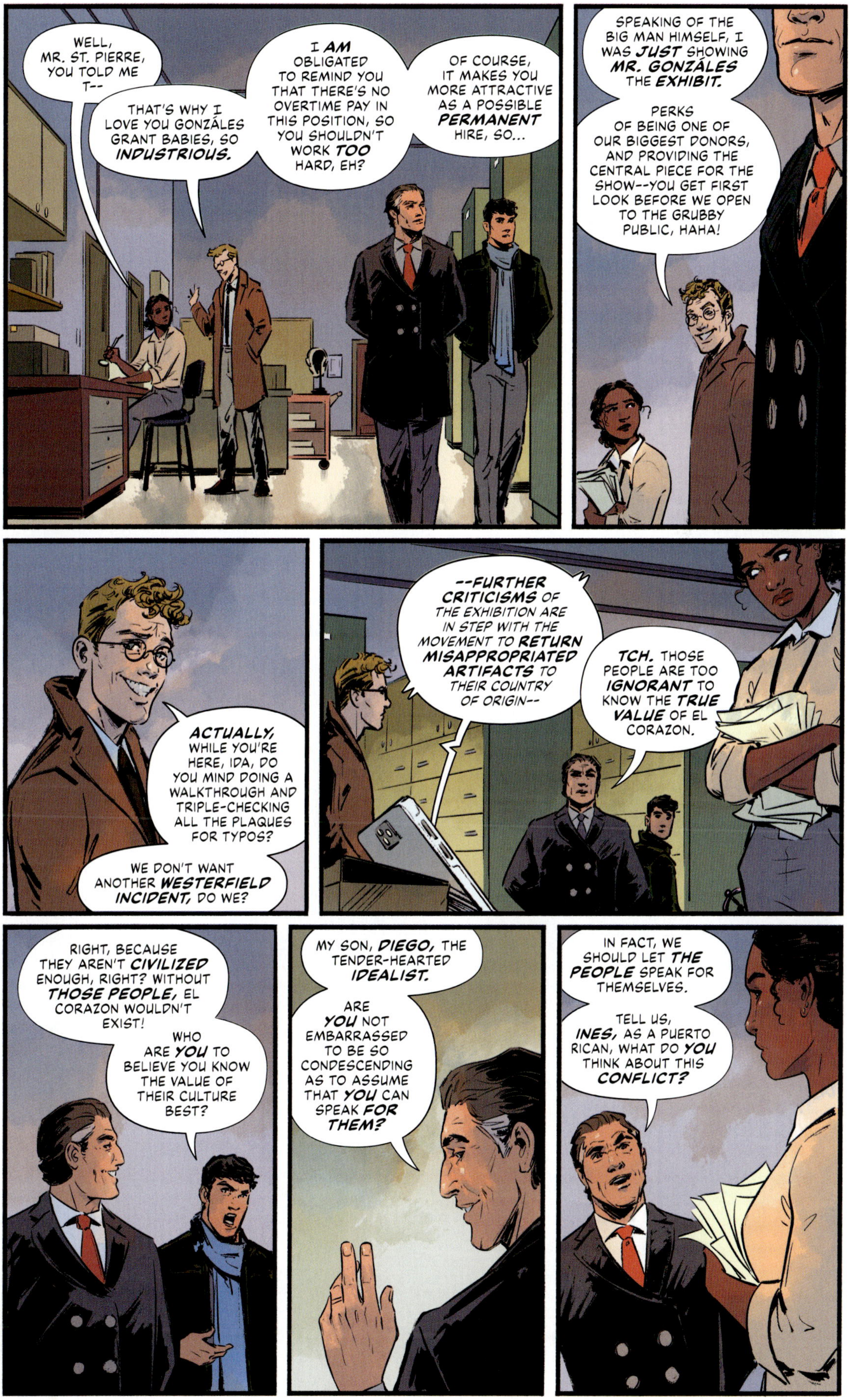
WELL, MR. ST. PIERRE, YOU TOLD ME T--
THAT'S WHY I LOVE YOU GONZÁLES GRANT BABIES, SO INDUSTRIOUS.
I AM OBLIGATED TO REMIND YOU THAT THERE'S NO OVERTIME PAY IN THIS POSITION, SO YOU SHOULDN'T WORK TOO HARD, EH?
OF COURSE, IT MAKES YOU MORE ATTRACTIVE AS A POSSIBLE PERMANENT HIRE, SO...
SPEAKING OF THE BIG MAN HIMSELF, I WAS JUST SHOWING MR. GONZÁLES THE EXHIBIT.
PERKS OF BEING ONE OF OUR BIGGEST DONORS, AND PROVIDING THE CENTRAL PIECE FOR THE SHOW--YOU GET FIRST LOOK BEFORE WE OPEN TO THE GRUBBY PUBLIC, HAHA!
ACTUALLY, WHILE YOU'RE HERE, IDA, DO YOU MIND DOING A WALKTHROUGH AND TRIPLE-CHECKING ALL THE PLAQUES FOR TYPOS?
WE DON'T WANT ANOTHER WESTERFIELD INCIDENT, DO WE?
--FURTHER CRITICISMS OF THE EXHIBITION ARE IN STEP WITH THE MOVEMENT TO RETURN MISAPPROPRIATED ARTIFACTS TO THEIR COUNTRY OF ORIGIN--
TCH. THOSE PEOPLE ARE TOO IGNORANT TO KNOW THE TRUE VALUE OF EL CORAZON.
RIGHT, BECAUSE THEY AREN'T CIVILIZED ENOUGH, RIGHT? WITHOUT THOSE PEOPLE, EL CORAZON WOULDN'T EXIST!
WHO ARE YOU TO BELIEVE YOU KNOW THE VALUE OF THEIR CULTURE BEST?
MY SON, DIEGO, THE TENDER-HEARTED IDEALIST.
ARE YOU NOT EMBARRASSED TO BE SO CONDESCENDING AS TO ASSUME THAT YOU CAN SPEAK FOR THEM?
IN FACT, WE SHOULD LET THE PEOPLE SPEAK FOR THEMSELVES.
TELL US, INES, AS A PUERTO RICAN, WHAT DO YOU THINK ABOUT THIS CONFLICT?

TO YOUR SON'S POINT, MR. GONZÁLES, THE CULTURAL CONTEXT OF AN ARTIFACT *IS* FOUNDATIONAL TO ITS VALUE...
I REMEMBER YOUR INITIAL APPLICATION TO MY FOUNDATION--I APPROVED IT MYSELF.
DID *YOU* NOT ESPOUSE THE IMPORTANCE OF 'SCRUPULOUS COLLECTORS' AND 'INSTITUTIONS OF ETHICAL CURATION' IN THE CONSERVATION OF ARTIFACTS?
WELL, YES, OF COURSE, WHAT I MEAN IS--
DON'T BULLY HER FOR NOT IMMEDIATELY AGREEING WITH YOUR INSULT TO HER CULTURE. *SHE'S* RIGHT.
THE *PEOPLE* ARE WHAT GIVE THEIR ART AND OBJECTS MEANING. WITHOUT THE CULTURAL CONTEXT, ANY ARTIFACT IS JUST A CURIO.
EITHER WAY, THIS IS AN INTELLECTUAL EXERCISE AT BEST.
EL CORAZON HAS BEEN IN THE FAMILY FOR *GENERATIONS.* IT IS *MINE.*
YES, EXCEPT IT WAS *STOLEN* FROM THE *TAINOS*--IT BELONGS TO THE PEOPLE OF *BORIKEN.*
TSK. BORIKEN.
IT WAS *NOTHING* BEFORE IT WAS PUERTO RICO.
THE PRIMITIVES OF THAT BACKWATER LITTLE COLONY THOUGHT THAT THE SPANIARDS WERE GODS.
THEY GAVE EL CORAZON TO *ME*--MY *ANCESTOR*--AS TRIBUTE, THEN GOT ANGRY WHEN THEY FINALLY REALIZED HE WAS JUST A MAN.
THEY DIDN'T THEN HAVE THE *CAPACITY* TO CHERISH SUCH AN ARTIFACT.
AT THIS POINT, IT IS MORE *MINE* THAN ANY OF THE MUDDLED HILLFOLK THEIR DESCENDANTS BECAME.
JESUS, DAD.

HA, WELL, TO BE FAIR, IF WE JUST GAVE BACK ARTIFACTS WILLY-NILLY, THE MUSEUM WOULD BE PRACTICALLY EMPTY, AND THOSE OBJECTS WOULD BE IN RUINS!
AND YOU KNOW WHAT THEY SAY--FINDERS, KEEPERS.
DESGRACIADO.
REGARDLESS, I CANNOT SIMPLY HAND OVER WHAT THEY WANT.
THIS PIECE, WHILE MESMERIZING, IS A RECREATION.
THE ORIGINAL NEVER LEAVES MY POSSESSION...
THE OLD MAN'S SENSES ARE FAILING HIM.
I SWAPPED THE ARTIFACT IN FOR THE VERY EXPENSIVE FAKE WHEN WE GOT HERE EARLIER.
THEY MAY BELIEVE IN "FINDERS, KEEPERS" BUT I AM MORE OF A "PUT UP OR SHUT UP" KIND OF MAN.
IF WE ARE TO "DO THIS" THEN THE LEAST WE CAN DO IS HONOR OUR COMMITMENT, HMM?

DO YOU DARE STEAL BACK EL CORAZON?

LEGEND TELLS THAT IF EL CORAZON IS ***NOT*** IN THE HEART OF EL YUNQUE WHEN THE GOD RETURNS, BORIKEN WILL ***SINK INTO THE SEA!*** YOU HEARD THIS STORY OFTEN GROWING UP, ENOUGH THAT IT MADE YOU WANT TO GO SEE IF YOU COULD ***FIND*** THE LOST ARTIFACT. AFTER YEARS AND YEARS OF INTENSE STUDY AND HARD WORK, YOU THINK YOU HAVE FINALLY FOUND YOUR PLACE IN THE WORLD – TO HELP MUSEUMS AND PUBLIC COLLECTIONS RESPECTFULLY ACQUIRE AND CONSERVE THEIR ARTIFACTS.

RULES

Find your way through the maze that is the museum and get to the **EXIT/ PARKING LOT** before you collect 3 alert counters!

ROLLS: move from room to room by rolling 2 six sided dice.

2 = success (move through door) + you may subtract 1 from next roll

3 = success (move through door + SUBTRACT 1 alert counter

4-6 = success (move through door)

7 = roll again + ADD 1 alert counter

8-10 = success (move through door + ADD 1 alert counter

11 = move BACK a space + ADD 1 alert counter

12 = automatic failure, go back to START

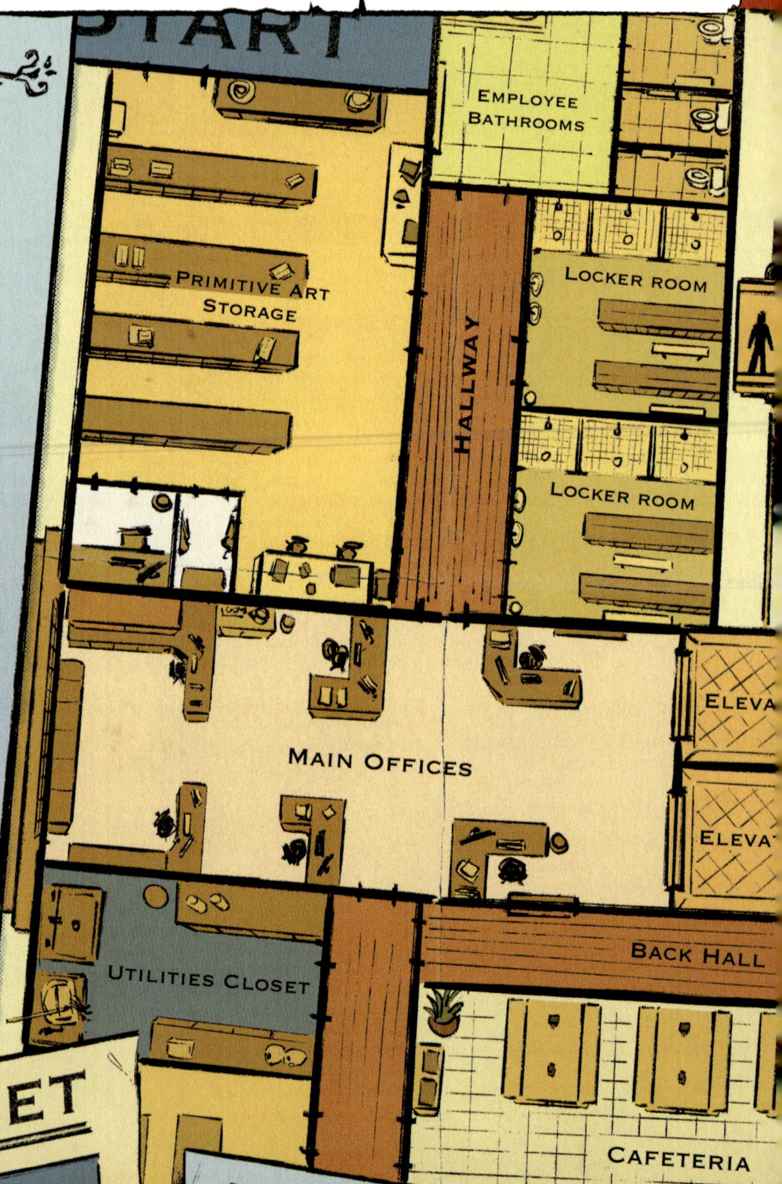

CTER SHEET

ROOM SCENARIOS *Read as you enter new areas!*

START: You begin in the PRIMITIVE ART STORAGE, where you have spent countless hours doing your boss's job for less than minimum wage. Move to the HALLWAY.

HALLWAY: You watch LEOPOLD disappear into the EMPLOYEE BATHROOMS down the hall – that was close! Move to the MAIN OFFICES.

MAIN OFFICES: A co-worker calls you over to ask how to log into their computer – they weren't supposed to be here! Add 1 alert counter. Choose PATH 1A or 2A.

TH 1A - ELEVATOR: Using the keycard lifted ffrom a co-worker's desk, you te the elevator. Move to PATH 2B.

PATH 2A. LOCKER ROOM: The JANITOR that likes you needs help moving a bench to clean. Only advance with a 2. Add 1 al counter, you subtract 1 from yo next roll, move to PATH 1B.

PATH 1B - EMPLOYEE BACK HALL: The JANITOR that doesr like you glares as you pass over where they are just finished mopping. Add 1 alert counter. Move to PATH 1C.

PATH 2B - "PRIMITIVE ART" galleries: You jump behind a large sculpture just as JUAN MIGUEL and TWO MEN storm past. JUAN MIGUEL looks furio but sick...Move to PATH 2C.

BUT JUST AS YOU BEGAN TO SETTLE IN, THE VERY THING THAT MADE YOU WANT TO SEE THE WORLD SHOWS UP ON YOUR DESK. YOU DON'T KNOW IF YOU BELIEVE THE LEGEND, BUT YOUR ***BLOOD*** IS ***CALLING*** FOR YOU TO RETURN WITH EL CORAZON TO YOUR HOMELAND. EXCEPT TO DO SO, YOU WOULD HAVE TO THROW AWAY EVERYTHING YOU HAVE WORKED FOR OVER THE LAST DECADE...
CLASSICAL PERIOD
ELEVATORS
PRIMITIVE ART
ELEVATORS
SCULPTURE GARDEN
OLD MASTERS
STAIRS
LOBBY
LOADING DOCK
END
PATH 1C - CAFETERIA: Your WORK HUSBAND offers you a snack. Roll 1 die – evens, remove 1 alert counter; odds you may subtract 1 from your next die roll. Move to PATH 1D.
PATH 2C - CLASSICAL PERIOD galleries: You chat with a patrolling SECURITY GUARD – they are used to seeing you leave here late at night. Move to PATH 2D.
PATH 1D - LOADING DOCK: Your favorite SECURITY GUARD is sneaking a smoke. Roll 2-7 = success - offer then a light and move on as they puff -- MOVE TO EXIT; 8-11 = move back 2 spaces - they ask to check your bag, but you "forgot something at the office;" 12 fail – you are caught!
PATH 2D - OLD MASTERS paintings: An after hours tour mistakes you for janitorial staff and hands you garbage to throw away. Smile or they will get suspicious – add an alert counter! Move to SCULPTURE GARDEN.
SCULPTURE GARDEN: Heavy footsteps behind you--jump behind a large marble statue! JUAN MIGUEL and the TWO MEN run past. Move to LOBBY.
LOBBY: The SECURITY GUARD at the checkpoint inspects your bag – only a 2 through 6 succeeds! A 7 through 11 sends you back 2 spaces a 12 fails and you are caught! Move to EXIT!

STOP HER! SHE HAS IT, I CAN FEEL IT!
SHOOT HER, YOU IDIOTS!
HEY, HEY--
SIN CARA.
HEY HEY, HO HO--
That way! Christ, all these vermin look the same.
I THINK SHE WENT THE OTHER WAY?
--YOU DON'T OWN WHAT YOU STOLE!

UGH!
HEY HEY, HO HO, YOU DON'T OWN WHAT YOU STOLE!
WHA--
'SCUSE ME!
HO HO--
SIN CARA!
--YOU DON'T OWN WHAT YOU STOLE!
Return Them!!
¡TRIPLE HIJUEPUTA!
HEY HEY, HO HO--
HEH.

BLAM
BLAM
BLAM
NOK
NOK
HOLA, ANA.
Ines?
It was *you* in my dreams?
I did it, Ana...
...I found it...

"In the time before we named this island, Yúcahu--god of the deep and fertile forest--touched a sacred tree, leaving behind a piece of his divinity at its heart.
"El Corazon del Yunque, a sacred object of lightning obsidian and living wood, was entrusted to the first Taino cacique.
"It was said that as long as El Corazon was cradled in the island's embrace, when Yúcahu returns every thousand years, the island would be protected from being engulfed by the fury of the sea.
"Lost to our people during the bloody massacre of 1511, it has not been seen since, and the next thousand-year mark is quickly approaching..."
Wait, it's gone?
But...does that mean we're gonna sink into the ocean?!
Not if I get it before the time runs out.
But... how can you, if no one knows where it is?
Ana, your gift's seeing, mine's finding.

See, I told you! I bet no one's seen that arrowhead in like a million years!
We'll be famous!
Famous, *eh?* What exactly does fame get you that you don't already have?
Whose affections are worth more than the duty you have to care for your people, and this Earth?
Now, give it here, Ines.
But, it's *mine.* I discovered it...
You did not *discover* anything, child. Discovery implies something was never known to begin with.
All you've done is *disturb* this poor woman's peaceful rest.
Those hunters' bones and tools have laid there for over 600 years, *put there* by loving hands.
Yes, Abuela.
Robbing graves and displaying their spoils is not better than respecting that things were placed with purpose, and leaving them there.
Not everything needs to be *consumed* to have meaning.
Give your *apologies* and *thanks* to your ancestors.
Like them, one day you will rest in the Earth, holding up the ground for your descendants to walk on.
Act from that knowledge, with the appropriate gratitude, and you will never act alone.
Hmph!

GASP
WHA--?! WHERE ARE WE?
The energy you brought with you screamed that we had to go.
Also you were shot, so I assume you are being pursued.
El Yunque... we have to get to El Yunque...
What is happening, Ines?
You disappear for years, then suddenly here you are, bleeding, smelling of trouble.
Start talking. Now.
If I knew you would be so intense, I would have called an Uber.
Oh no, you don't get to do that with me, Ines Guarua!
Not when I had to watch your grandmother waste away as she waited for you to come home, holding on and in agony as she watched the door for you.
Not when she went to her grave with your name on her lips.
I couldn't come home, Ana. Not after what I did...
Not until...
El Corazon. I found it.
And I'll return it to where it belongs, with hours to spare.
How?

"Museums, collectors, academics...they treat you like a tool, like you can't hear or see what is going on, like you can't ***think.***
"You're just furniture to them--no, ***less than,*** because they ***care*** about furniture."
YOU MIND FINISHING UP THE INTAKE FOR THE LATEST SHIPMENT, ***IDA?***
DON'T FORGET TO MOVE EL CORAZON TO THE STAGING AREA!
"All they do is ***take*** and ***claim*** and redistribute--they ***steal*** pieces of us, all in the name of '***preservation.***' And then they throw everything away like ***trash.***"
I can't believe I'm actually doing this...
Nestor, RU still organizin the protests outside the museum?
I need a favor...
all set. jus say the word.
this was A LOT on short notice. u owe me.
HEYYYYY INES. NEW CLOTHES? DID YOU JOIN JANITORIAL?
DID YOU GET A CHANCE TO DIGITIZE THE HERRMAN ACQUISITION RECORDS? AND THE PRESCOTT ACCOUNT STUFF, AND SMYTHE COLLECTION FILES I DROPPED OFF?
All those years I spent, studying and digging--paying for the ***privilege*** of ***working*** for ***them.*** I learned their ways too well--at this point, I know their system better than ***they*** do.
And then, ***there it was,*** right in front of me...
I could ***feel*** myself slipping away. Like I was disappearing into their emptiness.
I can't make everything right, and I don't even really know how much I ***believe*** in the legend...
...but I ***know*** Grandmother would have wanted me to bring it home before it was too late.
I saw it in my dreams... a figure with the shining, bleeding heart of the forest...I had no idea it would be ***you.***
Ines, I'm so--
KRUNCH

SCREEEEE
CHRIST! You okay?!
BANG
SHIT!
You need to stay down, Ines!
I know I was grazed earlier, but I'm not super acquainted with how to react when people are shooting at me!
Listen closely.
When I stop the car, you have to run--don't look back!
What? No, I can't leave you--
If you want us both to live, you have no choice!
I can distract them for a couple of minutes before I escape!
Take El Corazon and go. Fix this.
Ana, I... I--
Go now. The forest will guide you.
These bastards are mine.

SMASH
To return an object to a long-dead culture that would look down on you for your work?
"--GRAVE OF A **CHILD,** DEAD PROBABLY TO DISEASE. TRIBES LIKE THESE DIDN'T HAVE REAL MEDICINE...
You already had a prestigious internship, and yet it wasn't enough... what ***is it*** that you want?
A position at the Foundation, perhaps, to fund your ***personal projects?*** Tell me and it is yours...
REALLY, ***INA,*** THERE IS SO LITTLE LEFT WORTH EXPLORING IN THE ***PRIMITIVE*** AREAS OF FOCUS.
AS YOUR DISSERTATION ADVISOR, I REALLY FEEL I NEED TO STEER YOU TOWARD A ***REAL*** FUTURE--
It's over. You've nowhere to go now.
Unless... do you actually ***believe*** in that nonsense?
It's here... it's really here...zttt

Come now, Ines.
The artifact and I are *connected.*
You cannot keep it from me.
Why would you throw away the bright future you worked so hard for, eh?
...RELYING ON HERBS AND SUPERSTITIONS TO TREAT ILLNESS.
WHO WANTS TO SEE IF THEY CAN GUESS THE AGE FROM THE TEETH?
OH MAN, ARE THEY GONNA BE ROTTED THOUGH? WE KNOW THEY DIDN'T HAVE TOOTHBRUSHES, HAHA!
WHAT HAPPENS TO THE CHILD ONCE YOU FINISH THE DIG?
WELL, INES, THE *UNIVERSITY* WILL TAKE THE REMAINS AND EVERYTHING ELSE FOUND INTO THEIR COLLECTION.
THEY DIDN'T THEN HAVE THE *CAPACITY* TO CHERISH SUCH AN ARTIFACT...
Come now, girl, surely you've spent enough time around *civilized* people to be smarter than this!
No god walks here, and you are no hero of legend...
Give me the stone, girl. It has been *mine* longer than your muddy bloodline has dirtied this island.

Think carefully, girl. That was a gift, given to my family by the people here. They knew we deserved to have it.
You're alive, aren't you?
Like she always told me?
I know what you want. You want recognition-- I can give you that!
Keep your money. Keep your fucking fame.
Get off my goddamn island, you filthy thief!
NO!

GASP
WHO STANDS BEFORE ME?
You carry the heart of the forest, bearing it here from its wanders through strange and cruel lands. I know this, because the heart is mine.
But you, child, have hidden yourself from me. You have wandered farther even than what you have returned.
Are you of my people, or are you of his? Do you come for others, or for yourself?
...what... what does it all mean?
I...I don't even know what the heart is.
The heart is a gift--a covenant. A promise of wholeness.
When it is here, in its proper seat, it is the lifeblood of the people.
In the hands of a mortal, it extends the bearer's life by generations.
As he is no longer the bearer, this one is returning to his natural state.
Mortal men cannot evade the Earth forever.
This is crazy...

Your blood sings in the voice of this place, so I offer you the same choice I offered the First People.
Control the heart and live a long life of wealth and influence, passing it into your bloodline when the time comes--
--or protect and serve the land, giving your life for and to your People.
...your gift's seeing, mine's finding...
...we'll be famous...
...you're over 100 years old...
The things you've seen... the good that you could've done...
She doesn't get it, Ana. I have to go. If I stay here, I'm a nobody who'll never do anything.
I want to do something that matters. I want to be somebody.
You have always been someone to us--to me.
It's not enough.
All this--who I am if I stay--is not enough.
It's waiting out there for me to find, Ana. I know it.

ERR-ER-ER-ERRRK!
I thought you had slipped out the back for sure.
SNORT
This is my house.
The letters I sent you required confirmation signatures, so I know you got them. Let's talk about my offer.
No time wasted on even a "you look good for a dead woman."
You look great for a dead woman.
I'm...sorry about your father.
I loved my father, but he...was not a good man.
It breaks my heart that he hasn't been found yet, but I can't imagine whatever business he left on so suddenly was savory.
But you're deflecting.
Say yes, already.

I appreciate you helping keep my name out of the investigation of El Corazon's disappearance, Diego, but this is asking a *lot--*
From undergrad to your doctorate program, you've been essential personnel on digs, you've worked in museums, transporting artifacts, cataloging collections...
Literally no one knows the artifact trade better than you. And I'd bet no one *hates* it as much as you.
You know how exploitative, how *criminal* it all is.
So, help me make things right where we can.
Ines has already declined whatever it is you wanted her to be a part of.
What *more* do you *want,* Mr. Gonzáles?
My father was not a kind or generous man, I am the first to admit that, but he had one thing right, I think.
Being *custodians* of precious *cultural* artifacts is a calling. It makes a person *special.*
But there is no glory in stealing from people and charging them to see their property. There must be some sort of justice--reparation and restoration.
So, let's make things right. Let's take what the rich have stolen, and give it back to the people!
This sort of thing--planning what you are suggesting--it takes *time,* Diego. Time and *funding.*
Superheroing isn't cheap.
I'll clear my schedule.
THUNK

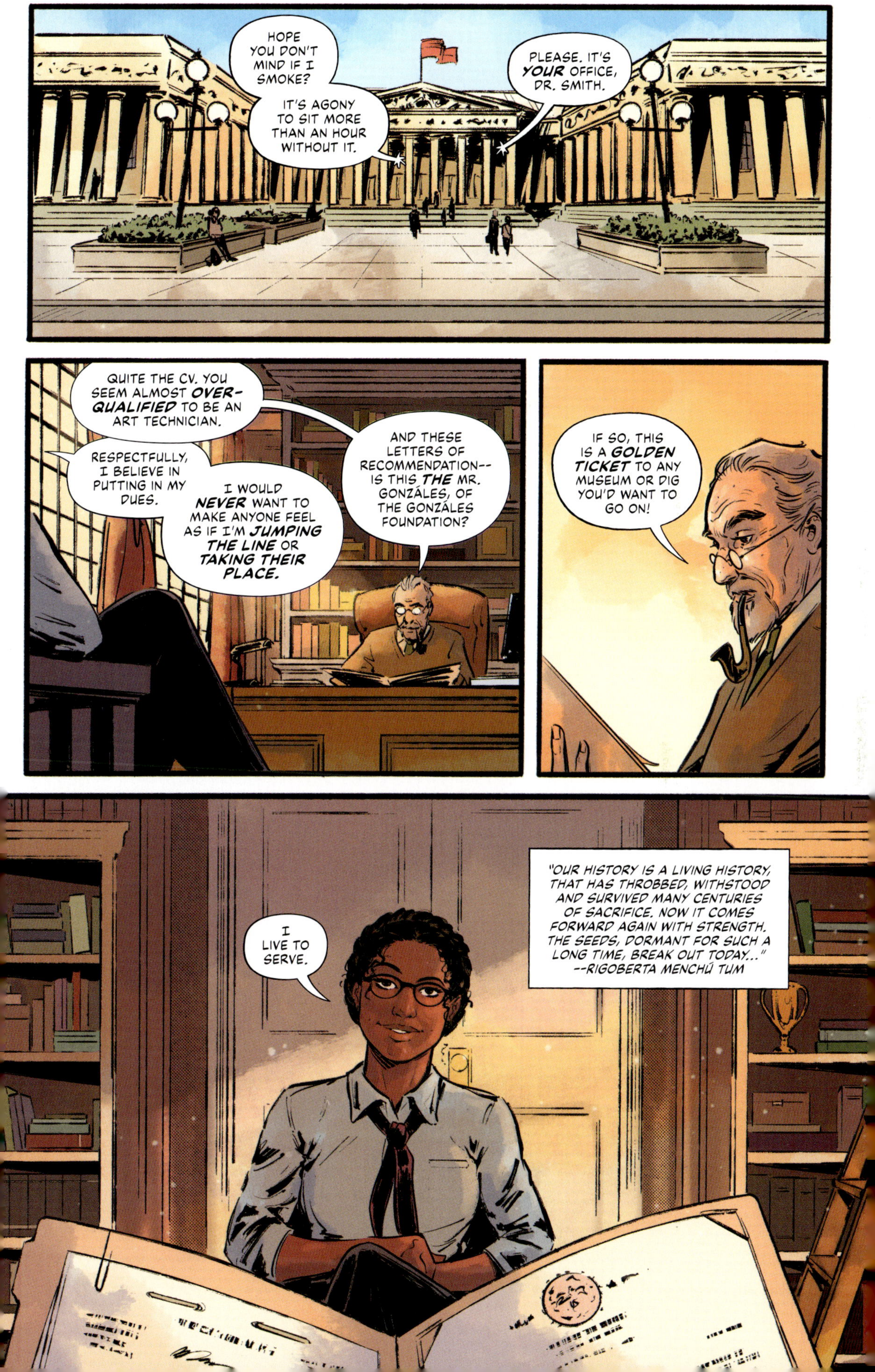
HOPE YOU DON'T MIND IF I SMOKE?
IT'S AGONY TO SIT MORE THAN AN HOUR WITHOUT IT.
PLEASE. IT'S YOUR OFFICE, DR. SMITH.
QUITE THE CV. YOU SEEM ALMOST OVER-QUALIFIED TO BE AN ART TECHNICIAN.
RESPECTFULLY, I BELIEVE IN PUTTING IN MY DUES.
I WOULD NEVER WANT TO MAKE ANYONE FEEL AS IF I'M JUMPING THE LINE OR TAKING THEIR PLACE.
AND THESE LETTERS OF RECOMMENDATION-- IS THIS THE MR. GONZÁLES, OF THE GONZÁLES FOUNDATION?
IF SO, THIS IS A GOLDEN TICKET TO ANY MUSEUM OR DIG YOU'D WANT TO GO ON!
I LIVE TO SERVE.
"OUR HISTORY IS A LIVING HISTORY, THAT HAS THROBBED, WITHSTOOD AND SURVIVED MANY CENTURIES OF SACRIFICE. NOW IT COMES FORWARD AGAIN WITH STRENGTH. THE SEEDS, DORMANT FOR SUCH A LONG TIME, BREAK OUT TODAY..." --RIGOBERTA MENCHÚ TUM

TARGET

"THE DAUGHTER OF THE DAWN" (upper half of statue)
large, solid stone. Will take equipment to move.

May need to damage slightly to get off the floor
(for repair, then take from conservation).

★ KEY CONTACTS/ENTRY POINTS

DR. C. SMITH - HEAD OF DEPT.
AT MUSEUM 30 YEARS. HAS ACCESS TO ARTIFACT, SCHEDULES FOR THE STAFF IN DEPT, ETC. MULTIPLE COMPLAINTS FROM FEMALE STAFF ABOUT HIM SKULKING AROUND THEIR LOCKER ROOM.

LETITIA BOLAJI - HEAD CUSTODIAN.
HAS ACCESS AND KEYS/CODES TO ALL AREAS OF THE MUSEUM, INCLUDING GARBAGE STORAGE AND LOADING DOCK AREAS. HAS SCHEDULES OF ALL AFTER HOURS STAFF.
HAS A PARTICULAR DISLIKE FOR DR. SMITH. WILL BE SYMPATHETIC TO HEARING HOW HE SUCKS, WILL PROBABLY BE VERY COMFORTING IF I NEED AN "EAR TO VENT TO."
GOOD WAY TO SET UP WHY I DISAPPEAR/QUIT.

O'CONNOR - SECURITY GUARD ON NIGHT SHIFT.
OPERATES THE LOADING DOCK DOOR MOST NIGHTS (4 SHIFTS A WEEK - 1 SHIFT ON THE INTERIOR OF THE BUILDING). SMART GUY, BUT VERY FRIENDLY - LESS ABLE TO BE MANIPULATED, BUT MORE TRUSTING IN GENERAL THAN REST OF SECURITY IN TERMS OF ALREADY VETTED STAFF. IN ANOTHER LIFE, WE WOULD BE FRIENDS.

HORACE WILLIAMS - HEAD CONSERVATOR FOR OIL PAINTINGS.
AT MUSEUM FOR 40 YEARS (STARTED AS A CLEANER). WORKS ODD HOURS (6PM TO 2AM). FRIENDLY, SCATTERED, INTELLIGENT BUT MYOPIC. WEALTH OF KNOWLEDGE ABOUT THE BUILDING, AND EVERYONE'S BUSINESS IN IT.

★ LOCATIONS

- DEPT. OFFICES - SEE ABOUT GETTING SCHEDULES FOR STAFF
- THE EXHIBIT - SECURITY ROUNDS AFTER CLOSING 3X A NIGHT - 10PM/2AM/5AM
- LOADING DOCK - SECURITY ROUNDS AFTER CLOSING 2X - 12AM/6AM
- BATHROOM JUST INSIDE THE LOADING DOCK - CLEANED AT 1:30AM NIGHTLY
- EMPLOYEE HALLWAYS - MODERATELY BUSY UNTIL 1AM, WHEN LAST OF NORMAL STAFF GONE

Once I have all the scheduling info, and have made friends with Horace and Letitia, arranging for the statue to be damaged (and so on a dolly in a less common area while waiting for repair) won't be hard. From there, timing a distraction for O'Connor and a delay in the dock for a delivery truck are simple, which should provide cover. They recently changed over to digital cameras, so a disrupting pattern on the face and clothing should keep me from being identified. Just have to figure out transportation for the statue from the museum to the docks.

I'M GONNA NEED SOME BACKUP ON THIS ONE...

FINDERS/KEEPERS, BUT WHAT ABOUT THE REST OF US?

Indiana Jones; Lara Croft; Rick O'Connell; and Evie Carnahan. Growing up in the '80s and '90s, I came up in a sort of golden age revival for the action/adventure genre. These characters and stories were exciting in a way that touches on something universal…

…except that, as a Black/Brown person, all that fun comes at the expense of peoples and cultures like mine. Is it wrong to love a genre that does not love me back?

For both the classic and the contemporary stories, in order to "have fun"/ "enjoy the adventure," Black and Brown people have to ignore the baked-in premise that we and our cultures are curiosities to be either plundered or else destroyed.

Raiders of the Lost Ark opens with Jones robbing an Indigenous temple of a religious artifact so important that the people who built the temple laid dozens of deadly traps to keep it safe. Why was Indy so determined to get the statue before the "villain" (who would sell it for money, so is a Bad Guy)? Because it "belongs in a museum." Not in the temple it was made for, or the people descended from its makers, but in a collection divorced from its context.

When Pornsak asked me to come up with a story that could only be told from the perspective of someone like me—a story that, should you change the particulars of the main character, the entire story would change—I immediately thought about these questions.

In attempting to answer them, and to get at the heart of where the thrill of these stories comes from, FINDERS/KEEPERS was born. A reverse Indiana Jones—a Brown woman who secrets away stolen artifacts from a museum to give them back to the people they were taken from.

I wanted to approach the culture (and so the artifact) as respectfully as possible. Even though the culture is my own, it felt wrong to use a real object.

FINDERS/KEEPERS means to flip not just the characters, but to flip the idea of where the legitimacy of the hero comes from. It is meant to invite those of us that have always been the stock character—comedic sidekick, the exotic seductress, the savage barbarian—to be the fully realized protagonist. This story is an invitation for us to take back what was stolen from us, and to do it with style. And in that, it is an invitation for us to finally fully understand that thing that makes the action/adventure genre so damn fun.

This is the kind of story that could go on a long time, but is designed for each adventure to be satisfying. Even as I was writing it, multiple countries were calling on both the Metropolitan Museum of Art and the British Museum to return their sacred art.

What kinds of people—both enemy and ally—will Ines encounter as she continues on her adventures? What did she really see in the rain forest, as she bled her way up the mountain? What new cultures and artifacts will she learn about as she attempts to right these wrongs? What kinds of trouble will she fall into along the way?

The ending of the issue is a call for readers to join Ines on her quest, and find out…

Vita Ayala

Vita

TULA LOTAY VARIANT COVER ART